Ministry for A New Time

JAMES C. FENHAGEN
with Celia Allison Hahn

Ecumenical Reflections by
Michael Cooper-White
Arthur Gafke
Mary V. Atkinson
Davida Foy Crabtree

Study Guide by Jean M. Haldane

Published by The Alban Institute, Inc.
in cooperation with
The Cornerstone Project
A Ministry of the Episcopal Church Foundation

11/96

The Publications Program of The Alban Institute is assisted by a grant from Trinity Church, New York City.

Library of Congress Catalog Number 95-78601
ISBN #1-56699-156-0

V
52.1
4
995
,1

CONTENTS

Foreword   v

Acknowledgments   ix

Introduction   xi

Chapter 1. Leadership in an Era of Turbulence   1
            Ecumenical Reflections   19

Chapter 2. A Profile of Episcopal Clergy   24
            Ecumenical Reflections   39

Chapter 3. Rethinking Our Theologies of Ordination   45
            Ecumenical Reflections   61

Chapter 4. The Bishop and the Diocese in a Time of Change: 68
            Reconnecting Function and Symbol in the Episcopal
            Church
            Ecumenical Reflections   80

Chapter 5. The Case for Systemic Change   86
            Ecumenical Reflections   101

Chapter 6. The Spiritual Roots of Christian Leadership   110
            Ecumenical Reflections   124

Appendix. A Case Study Method   129

Notes   132

Your Dialogue with Ministry for a New Time   137
Study Guide

FOREWORD

Jim Fenhagen here presents a "case study for change" from the Episcopal experience which tells how one communion is seeking to join tradition and contemporary experience to strengthen ordained ministry for a new time. There is much about this book that I find helpful; here I want to emphasize two ways Jim's work seems to me especially on target.

One has to do with tradition—the emphasis on reclaiming the spiritual roots that alone can ground clergy, can help them stand steady and move sturdily ahead into challenging times. We need to rediscover *corporate* forms of spirituality—and one major place to rediscover them is in the *leaders' role*.

My other primary source of excitement about this book has to do with the way the discussion keeps reaching out beyond the church to the world-now for which the church exists (an imperative too often forgotten by the ecclesiastically absorbed) where broader, more creative conversations are desperately needed to replace the win-lose debates that polarize us and breed mutual contempt but do not reveal helpful next steps.

This book aims to be one step toward that broader conversation of which Fenhagen speaks. It aims to live out right here in these pages that more embracing dialogue for which we long. In good traditional Alban practical ecumenical style, and in order to open up the discussion about where clergy are today and how we need to envision ordained ministry for the future, I asked colleagues in the United Church of Christ, Evangelical Lutheran Church in America, United Methodist Church, and Presbyterian Church (USA) to recommend some responders to Jim Fenhagen's study of Episcopal clergy. Davida Foy Crabtree (UCC), Conference Minister, Southern California Conference, United Church of Christ; Michael Cooper-White (ELCA), Director, Department for

Synodical Relations/Conference of Bishops, and assistant to the Bishop of the ELCA; Arthur Gafke (UMC), Director of Supervision and Support Systems, Division of Ordained Ministry, Board of Higher Education and Ministry; and Mary V. Atkinson (PCUSA), formerly Associate Director, Church Vocations Ministry Unit, now retired, were highly recommended as experts on the clergy scene by their denominational colleagues and all agreed to respond to questions put by the author:

1. What in this chapter did you find most stimulating?

2. In what ways are the issues raised in this chapter similar to what you experience in your denomination and in what ways are there noticeable differences?

3. What common learnings, challenges, or questions stimulated by this chapter do we together have to share with the whole church?

As you can see, each responder came at the task in a unique way, and as Jim and I scratched our heads about how to integrate such helpful but disparate comments, it occurred to me that it was as though he had presented an Episcopal "case study," and his fellow-learners from four other major mainline denominations were responding to the case he presented and adding reflections from their experiences in their own faith traditions.

So, following each chapter, I will present some of the "case study group's" comments and lift up especially those that seem to me to suggest some common concerns mainline churches might like to ponder as they think about "the future shape of ministry." I'll serve as convener of our case study group and add a few reflections from my own standpoint as one who has listened in on clergy issues from Alban's ecumenical perspectives over the last twenty years.

You might make use of the "case" and the "case study group" by forming a case study group of your own—a clergy group (within your denomination or including a group of local clergy), a judicatory committee (such as a commission or committee on ministry), or an educational venture that brings together clergy and lay leaders from a number of churches.

The case study in this book will get your conversation started; go with the momentum and launch into your own discussion. How do the issues in each chapter take shape in our own life and ministry? (Here you may find it useful to prepare your own case studies from your experience in ministry and present them to your colleagues. See the appendix for sample instructions.) Does any vision emerge for us about how we might move toward more faithful and effective ministry for the world for which our church is given? What would be some first steps toward walking into that vision? Now what would we like to communicate to our "persistent friends"—our middle or national judicatory executives—or across denominational lines through The Alban Institute?* You're on your way in your own "case studies for change"!

Celia A. Hahn

*Write for Alban article guidelines.

ACKNOWLEDGMENTS

My two years with the Cornerstone Project have been a time of incredible learning and hope. I am grateful for the vision of Peter Megargee Brown, George Fowlkes, and Jeff Kittross of the Episcopal Church Foundation, who helped bring Cornerstone into being; for Loren Mead, Barry Evans, and Roy Oswald, who have served as consultants and wisdom figures along the way; for Bill Andersen, Saundra Richardson, and my other colleagues on the Foundation staff; for Alan and Billie Houghton, Eulalie Fenhagen, and Holly Hollerith, who have read and critiqued these chapters along the way; and for that incredible hands-on group of talented and faithful people on the Cornerstone board, who, with our many partners throughout the church, have made it possible for a few people to accomplish a lot.

My expressions of gratitude for the many people who in one way or another have shared in this book would not be complete without acknowledging my indebtedness to Michael Cooper-White, of the Evangelical Lutheran Church in America; Davida Crabtree, of the United Church of Christ; Arthur Gafke, of the United Methodist Church; and Mary V. Atkinson, of the Presbyterian Church (USA). Drawing on their long experience in the field of ministry development, these four offer comments on what I have written; they give the perspective of what is happening in their denominations. I am deeply grateful for their wisdom and their help.

None of this would have happened, however, without the vision and initiative of Celia Hahn, editor in chief of The Alban Institute, who edited the ecumenical comments and tied them to each book chapter, and Jean Haldane, a total ministry advocate par excellence, who wrote the study guide.

And finally I give thanks for the wisdom of the board of the Episcopal Church Foundation to maintain its commitment to the Cornerstone vision in appointing William Craddock, a warm and thoughtful lay member of the church, to continue on with what has been begun.

INTRODUCTION

In the spring of 1987, Peter Megargee Brown, then president of the board of the Episcopal Church Foundation, met with Edmond Browning, the presiding bishop of the Episcopal Church, in what was to become the beginning of a major new initiative marking a turning point in the Foundation's history. The Episcopal Church Foundation is an independent board of Episcopal laity who over the years have raised money for special projects within the Episcopal Church. Peter Brown went to see the presiding bishop with one question on his mind: What new concern should the Episcopal Church Foundation address as it prepares for the next century?

Edmond Browning's reply was direct. He hoped the Foundation would make effectiveness and spiritual well-being among the clergy its top priority.

This conversation, confirmed by many similar conversations with leaders throughout the denomination, resulted in a major Foundation initiative to build stronger systems of support for clergy and their families. A September 1987 planning meeting brought together a group with wide experience working with clergy, tasked to design a plan that would enable the Foundation to get started. The first step was to contract with Loren Mead, founder of The Alban Institute, and Barry Evans, director of the Grubb Institute, to conduct a nationwide study of the clergy of the Episcopal Church that would address issues of morale, effectiveness, emotional and spiritual health, and vocational clarity. The study, titled "Excellence in Ministry: The Personal and Professional Needs of the Clergy of the Episcopal Church," completed in 1989, became the basis of the Foundation's response, a project initially called Excellence in Ministry and soon tagged the Cornerstone Project.

For the past twenty years, the creative and progressive energy of the Episcopal Church has been centered around the recovery of the ministry of the laity. The books and articles read and discussed have for the most part been books that affirmed the communal and nonhierarchical nature of the church given to us in baptism and affirmed in an understanding of the Eucharist, where the priesthood of the people of God stands at the center of the church's self-offering in Christ. The theological problem that has emerged as a result of our increasing clarity about the ministry of the laity is an increasing lack of clarity about the ministry of the clergy. The truth is that we are living in a theological time lag. Our theology of baptism reflects a vision of the church that is in conflict with our theology of ordination and the structures and symbols by which this theology is communicated.

The renewal and support of the ordained leadership of the church is more than a matter of teaching new skills or creating situations that help clergy feel good about themselves. Renewal is fundamentally a theological issue involving a radical transformation in our understanding of who we are and what it is we are called to be and do as ordained members of the baptized community of faith. Ordination is a gift of the church on behalf of the church. The structures that support our understanding of ministry (organization, language, titles, authority) need to be structures that re-enforce mutuality, collegiality, shared commitment, servanthood in the use of power, and life in Christ given to us in baptism and celebrated in the Eucharist. As we embrace this emerging paradigm given to us by the Holy Spirit, the vacuum that now exists in the church will be filled.

The concerns of this book are the concerns that have emerged as a result of Cornerstone's engagement with the clergy and laity of the Episcopal Church over the past five years. We see many changes taking place in the denomination both in theology and practice, as the Episcopal Church engages in the often painful process of redefinition. This book is an exploration from many angles of this process of redefinition. Its purpose is to begin a conversation that we hope might extend beyond the Episcopal Church to those many other church bodies that share similar concerns. To help broaden this conversation, we have asked four people known for their interest and experience in working with clergy to comment on what I have written from their perspective and the theology and practice of the denominations to which they belong. Are the changes taking place in the ministry of the Episcopal Church common to all, and, if so, how? In sharing our similarities and differences, I trust we might discover at a deeper level what we need to learn from one another.

This small book, *Ministry for a New Time: Case Study for Change*, is a report, written for a broad audience, of what we have learned about clergy well-being in a particular denominational context. From what I have read and heard from colleagues in other denominations, the problems and concerns are remarkably similar. It is hoped that this book might build on Loren Mead's seminal book *The Once and Future Church* and serve as a stimulus for discussion and action both on the local and judicatory levels. The recovery of the authority of the ministry of the laity has brought new vitality and vision to the life of the church. Unless this vitality and vision can be reinforced and built into the life of the church and marketplace, our hard-won gains will be lost. It is our conviction that this is what the ordained ministry is called to do, not as those standing apart but as partners in mission sharing a common task as a sign of Christ's presence in the community of faith.

In one way or another, this book is about leadership in the new paradigm that Mead describes in his book. Its focus is on the clergy of the Episcopal Church as one point of entry into a particular system. Forces at work in the church, which in most cases are also reflected in the world around us, raise particular concerns about the kind of leadership the church will need for the future. In one way or another, what follows in this book will seek to address these concerns. I note some of these as questions for further exploration:

- How can the church as a system give greater priority to reinforcing the gifts of clergy who are motivated and committed to growth and less time to crisis intervention?
- What process needs to be established that will enable the church to distinguish between symbols that empower and symbols that block mission so as to produce motivation for change?
- What needs to be done to move us beyond isolation and competitiveness to the building of systems that both connect and support?
- What kind of structures can be made available to encourage self-assessment and the spiritual and physical disciplines that contribute to better health and the deepening of life in Christ?

These are not easy issues to address, but they are issues of immense importance to the mission of the church. As this book seeks to point out, this particular time in history has presented us with a challenge to move beyond our internal bickering to begin anew the task of systemic change. This book is offered as a contribution to the discussion that must undergird whatever response is made—in the conviction that the Holy Spirit is really at work among us.

James C. Fenhagen

CHAPTER 1

Leadership
in an Era of Turbulence

In a fascinating article titled "Lashed to the Mizzen: Leadership in an Era of Turbulence" (from which I have taken the title of this chapter), Bernie Ghiselin makes some interesting comments about trends affecting leadership in the U.S. business community today. Ghiselin's comments also have a lot to say about leadership in the church, particularly with regard to the church that is emerging.

"However turbulence is defined," Ghiselin writes, "the old models of leadership and management, conceived at times when organizations faced different problems, are inadequate.... Coordination and teamwork are among managers' most difficult challenges, not only at operating levels, but throughout the hierarchy."[1]

What makes sense for the business community in our time does not necessarily make sense for the Christian church. But what does make sense is the reality of the change that is taking place in our world and the demand for a new kind of leadership that this change requires. The church is not exempt from this demand.

The Changing Shape of Religion in America

If there was any doubt that religion was re-emerging as a shaping force in American society, this doubt was dispelled by the elections of 1994. Religion, particularly conservative Christianity, is alive and well in the public arena. In *The Culture of Disbelief*, a widely read commentary on the contemporary interaction of religion and culture, Stephen L. Carter notes that "contemporary American politics faces few greater dilemmas

than deciding how to deal with the resurgence of religious belief."[2]
Using the First Amendment to the U.S. Constitution as his stepping
stone, Carter urgently argues that the church (meaning all churches) must
make a more aggressive public witness for the recovery of those values
—justice and compassion and civility—about which people of faith can
agree. What we are seeing, however, seems to be the exact opposite of
Carter's call. In the current debate over religious values in the public
realm, the values of justice and compassion and civility seem most diminished. This indicates that the resurgence of religion can bring both
threat and promise. Unless churches that historically have honored exploration and openness as a doorway to faith are aggressive in their witness to a more inclusive center, much of what has been gained toward
greater religious tolerance and compassion will be lost for a long time to
come.

In his book *Christianity in the Twenty-First Century,* Robert
Wuthnow clearly warns about the serious threat reflected in the dark side
of the fundamentalism that fuels the religious right. "Perhaps to a degree
more evident than in most other systems of belief," Wuthnow writes,

> fundamentalism is thus a framework in which polarities abound.
> The believer exists in a world of right and wrong, good and evil,
> light and darkness, mammon and God, flesh and spirit, demons and
> angels, worldly temptations and heavenly salvation.... As we move
> into the twenty-first century, we are likely to find fundamentalist
> hatred shifting toward other targets, such as Muslims, environmen-
> talists, the New Age movement, or politicians of certain parties.[3]

The problem, of course, is not only what impact this will have on the
already strained fabric of American society, but also on those divisions
that are already present in the "mainline churches" themselves. At a time
when the door is once again being opened for the church to play its part
in the rebuilding of a deeply troubled society, the nature of its witness is
a matter of enormous consequence. "Secular liberals," writes Stephen
Carter,

> have rarely appreciated and have never seemed sympathetic to what
> Falwell (and his Moral Majority) instinctively understood: the
> powerful sense of America spinning out of control in ways that are

for many religious people, profoundly threatening. What is needed, especially from liberals who pride themselves on a politics of inclusion, is a dialogue that takes these fears seriously, a dialogue that teaches but also tries to learn.[4]

This same kind of dialogue must take place within the church as well. Our capacity to move beyond the divisions that now dominate the life of the church will determine our capacity to embrace the promise that the Spirit holds before us. Leadership for tomorrow must be prepared to enter into this dialogue with sensitivity and wisdom.

With these words still in my mind, I picked up my morning paper *(Myrtle Beach Sun Times)* and was struck by an op-ed column by William Raspberry of the *Washington Post*. Raspberry's article, titled "Religious Right Acts as a Tribe," wrestled with the way power is used by religious institutions to influence public policy, contrasting the witness of the church in the Civil Rights struggle with the witness of the "religious right" in our day. "Is there a principled difference between the two uses of religious based power?" Raspberry asks. He thinks there is and he bases his discussion on an image he discovered in a booklet by Don E. Eberly, titled *Restoring the Good Society.* Eberly made a distinction between tribesmen and citizens. Eberly and Raspberry agreed that the religious right works on a tribal model that reinforces fear and anger.

Quoting Eberly, Raspberry expands his insight further:

> Tribal politics encourages methods of action that are designed to produce tribal solidarity so as to counter the assault coming from the outside.... The more compelling model for public participation is the citizen model. Here the church is simply called to serve society, not as conditions require but because of God's demands. Politics is thus but one facet of this calling. The citizen translates belief into a public philosophy, seeks to build inclusive coalitions around a broad agenda, and prefers persuasion to polarization.[5]

Eberly's words, which so caught Raspberry's attention, reflect a growing body of thought aimed at building a new point of connection between church and society that will open us, rather than close us off, to the emerging future. In different ways, Stephen Carter and Robert Wuthnow are arguing for the same thing. The quest for a new moral

center is the social agenda that lies at the heart of the church's mission
now and in the years to come.

The Promise That Is Before Us

For the past decade, the engagement of theology and culture that so
dominated the Episcopal Church in the late fifties and early sixties has
given way to institutional concerns reflective of the concerns that dominate the culture. These institutional concerns seemed to be addressed as
if the culture were the enemy. We talked about engaging the culture,
indeed, even transforming the culture (to use H. Richard Niebuhr's now-
classic categories), but deep down at the grassroots level, we were, and
I believe still are to a greater extent than we would like to believe, a
church against culture, afraid to trust what might be movements of the
Spirit that are stronger in the "world" than in the church. Sometimes it
seems as if we are more concerned with holding our fingers in the dike
than discerning the presence of God in the water.

I do not in any sense want to diminish the importance of the debates
that continue to take place in the Episcopal Church, of which I am a part,
over the Prayer Book, the ordination of women, and issues of sexuality,
particularly homosexuality. These issues and the interpretation of Scripture regarding them need to be discussed and debated. What concerns
me is not the disagreement we are experiencing over these issues, but our
unwillingness to let the Holy Spirit lead us beyond our seeming "stuck-
ness." As a denomination we have been preoccupied with proving who
is right and who is wrong, without trusting the Spirit to lead us into a
new truth that lies beyond or beneath what we now know. The energy
and the anger we have expended as a denomination over these differences have dominated our life for almost a quarter of a century and distorted the vision of that mission to which we are being called.

Maybe even more far-reaching than our internal squabbles, however,
is the loss of that ecumenical spirit that once energized our witness to the
Gospel in the world. Conversations among the Episcopal Church and
other church bodies still go on, but, with one or two notable exceptions,
very few people take them very seriously. As a result, we present to the
world a church that is as fractured and disconnected as the world is. The
vision that lies behind the ecumenical movement is more than the need

for churches to cooperate. It is a theological statement about the redemptive activity of God. The Christian church is by its very nature a sign of the unity of God and of the interconnectedness of all things and of all people in Christ. Not to be serious about Christian unity is not to be serious about the Gospel. When we take the culture seriously, we are drawn into connection with others with whom we need to work and from whom we need to learn. It doesn't take any special gift of faith to be grasped by the fact that God cares far less about the Episcopal Church and its future than God cares about the healing of the brokenness of the world.

At a recent meeting of the Consortium of Endowed Episcopal Parishes, Diogenes Allen, a faculty member at Princeton Theological Seminary, made some interesting comments about the nationwide shift in the way religion is being seen by the culture. The "uphill struggle to make Christianity credible in a hostile intellectual climate is over," he stated. "We are now on a much more level playing field. This is not yet generally known among intellectuals both in and outside the church, but the change is easily documented." And if you are at all familiar with some of the discussion going on in the realm of physics and the environmental sciences, you have a sense of what Allen is referring to. His concern, however, is that the church has been so self-preoccupied for so long that we might well miss the opportunity at hand.

"Our spiritual condition is such," he continues, "that we lack the energy and knowledge to respond to the new age, a postmodern one, that we are entering. . . . I submit that one of the main features of the spiritual condition of the Episcopal Church can be captured by a single word, *accedie*."[6] *Accedie* Allen defines as a pervasive sense of discouragement, even cynicism, about the capacity of the church to make its witness in the world; this attitude, of course, can be a self-fulfilling prophecy. *Accedie* is a spiritual issue because it is essentially a loss of hope. We become preoccupied with our apparent lack of what the world defines as success; in that preoccupation, we don't trust fully in the redemptive power of God to renew the church of Christ and the world as well. This is the Gospel message. In Christ the victory has been won. Through the power of his resurrection, Jesus Christ has overcome those powers that would destroy the world.

If for a moment you are tempted to think that God has given up on us, take a look at what has happened in South Africa. In the powerful and almost unbelievable reconciling witness made by Nelson Mandela

and Frederick De Klerk, we have been given a sign of God's redemptive
activity in the world. De Klerk himself said it: "A power greater than
man has given South Africa the spirit, the chance to go forward in peace."
When Nelson Mandela, after twenty-seven years in prison as an enemy
of the state, reached out to shake the hand of President De Klerk and the
two embraced, we saw before our eyes the miracle of God's reconciling
love. Five years before, who would have imagined it possible?

The Emergence of a New Paradigm

Signs of God's kingdom breaking into contemporary life are not new in
human history, but the way we view these signs varies radically, depending on the spiritual lens through which we view them. In his challenging
and widely read book *The Once and Future Church,* Loren Mead makes
a compelling case for the emergence of what more and more people now
refer to as a new paradigm. Only through the new lens provided by a
paradigm shift are we able to understand the forces at work in the church
that demand our response. These forces are both internal and external
and include not only forces that emerge from the culture, but also forces
inspired and shaped by the Holy Spirit. "Changes of paradigm are, by
definition, matters of perception, feeling, world view, consciousness,"
Mead writes.

> They are not external changes like the leveling of a mountain. As a
> result, one of the most difficult realities we deal with is the fact that
> two people, living side by side, may face the same phenomenon, yet
> their perceptions may differ radically.[7]

We don't have to look very far to see how true this is.

In looking at the role of the clergy in this emerging church, as this
book seeks to do, I am interested in exploring not only what new demands are being made of the clergy, but also what this says about the
way clergy need to understand themselves and their vocations if they are
to minister effectively in that future that is upon us. In line with that objective, I've woven throughout these chapters about the ordained ministry within the Episcopal Church a series of biases that represent ways of
looking at the current paradigm shift. Some of these have been widely

spoken of and are central to the way many thoughtful people are beginning to speak about the Christian church today. Others are more exploratory and have surfaced for me as a result of the Cornerstone Project and what we have learned.

In what follows I would like to lift up six such biases and develop them to the point where they might serve as a lens through which we might better understand (1) what is happening to clergy today and (2) what these learnings tell us about the systemic changes that are needed if, as a church, we are to minister effectively. I have given titles to the six paradigm biases I see as being of particular importance to the church's ministry and mission:

- the kingdom of God in our midst;
- thinking globally, acting locally;
- the new laity;
- the centrality of the small-group experience;
- scriptural authority and interpretation;
- leadership for a new paradigm.

The Kingdom of God in Our Midst

The kingdom of God is a vision of what God created the world to be. It is a vision that according to God's plan will ultimately be realized in full, the signs of which are present in the world now, like mustard seed or leaven. The many often-disconnected pictures the Bible gives us of Jesus' ministry are what we might call snapshots of the kingdom of God. They tell us in story form how God interacts with human history and, when linked together, present us with an outline of a world where the values that we take for granted are often turned upside down. Only through eyes of faith sharpened by the gift of discernment are we able to see that kingdom in our midst.

As we look at the world around us with a discerning heart, we can see many things and events that reinforce this kingdom vision of which the scriptures speak. "Look at the fig tree and all the trees," Jesus said to his disciples, "as soon as they sprout leaves you can see for yourselves and know that summer is already near. So also, when you see these things taking place, you know that the kingdom of God is near" (Luke

21:29–31). Consider a few contemporary snapshots that would suggest we cannot understand what is happening without looking through a theology-of-the-kingdom lens: The concern in our world for the building of human community that transcends difference of race and class is a kingdom concern. Our struggle with what Walter Wink calls the "powers of domination" is a kingdom concern. Our newfound stewardship of the earth is a kingdom concern. Our concern over the fate of the world's children and the increasing gap between rich and poor is kingdom-related. All these suggest that undergirding the emerging paradigm is a theology of the kingdom of God that we must grasp anew if we are to be faithful in our discipleship. Not only was the preaching of the kingdom of God central to Jesus' ministry, but it is also the theological truth that affirms God's victory over the power of sin in the world through Jesus' death and the triumph of his resurrection. "In the world you have tribulation," Jesus told his disciples, "but be of good cheer, I have overcome the world" (John 16:33 RSV).

This victory is the source of Christian hope. The kingdom of God has come, and through the ultimate working out of this victory in the world, the dominion of God will be fulfilled in human history. We affirm this reality in the eucharistic proclamation, "Christ has died. Christ is risen. Christ will come again." It might well be that the work of the Spirit in the world that demands our attention is God's way of calling the church anew to that kingdom vision that alone points us to the unity we seek.

Thinking Globally, Acting Locally

This bumper sticker slogan has been around for a long time, but never has it been so true as it is today. In the Episcopal Church we have moved from an authority, expressed through an international sense of what it meant to be a part of the Anglican Communion, to diocesan authority vested in a bishop, to what now is a sense of authority that begins on the local level and works outward. The shift in authority began as the autonomous national churches of the Anglican Communion developed liturgies that expressed the particularities of their faith and practice. It was once said that the authority of the Anglican Communion over its member churches was enshrined in *The Book of Common Prayer*. No matter how different we were, we prayed the same. Although the outward forms of the Prayer Book reflect a common heritage, the freedom of national churches to make widely varied liturgical changes diminished the sense of common authority. So when the Episcopal Church in the United States made the decision to ordain women to the priesthood and episcopate, the old argument that this could not happen without the consent of the entire Communion no longer held true.

The same shift has happened on the national and diocesan level as well, with implications of immense consequence for the shape and stewardship of the Church's mission throughout the world. The authority once bestowed upon the presiding bishop and the executive council of the Episcopal Church in the United States has shifted to the local bishop and the diocese and is granted by the local congregation. There was a time when being ordained as a bishop in the Episcopal Church assured the granting of authority that everyone recognized and respected. As is obvious in all spheres of life, those days are gone forever. The authority that engenders respect and trust must be won; the people in the congregations give their bishops or moderators or conference ministers this authority. Only then is this authority confirmed by the office itself. It is not always an easy process. It takes time and immense effort on everyone's part; it can easily be lost, but it is the process by which effective leadership is built.

Given this reality, however, the fact remains that a global not a parochial vision is a mark of the new paradigm. The economic and political structures that most affect our lives are global structures, and it is through this global vision expressed in the life of the church that we bear witness to the reality of the kingdom of God.

One of the farthest reaching systemic interventions to occur in the life of the Episcopal Church in the last few decades was the call to "Mutual Responsibility and Interdependence in the Body of Christ" that emerged from the General Convention meeting in St. Louis in 1964. This convention gave birth to the worldwide partnerships that now link the Anglican Communion on a people-to-people basis. This system of partnership is still in place after thirty years and continues to play a major part in shaping the vision that undergirds the Communion's mission. What happens in Rwanda or Haiti does indeed affect what happens in the Communion in every other part of the world, for if one part of the body of Christ suffers, we all suffer together. This reality is at the heart of the

Church's mission because it describes what and who we are as the *people of God* in this time and place.

Two manifestations of this global vision have taken on new energy in our day: (1) the expansion of partnership programs on the local level and (2) the rapid growth of intercultural ministry in the United States. The acts of compassion that have come out of international partnerships have transformed the daily lives of thousands of people. Even more locally, the rapidly growing emphasis on multicultural ministries throughout the Episcopal Church in the United States has begun to bring home the fact that globalism is not something far away but a reality of our common life. This call to a multicultural vision is at the heart of the church's mission in the twenty-first century.

In speaking of the church in the twenty-first century, Robert Wuthnow argues that we can be certain that "denominational identity will in practice mean a *local* identity. . . . Truly national organizations, such as political parties, are eroding in their ability to retain people's loyalties, just as denominations are."[8] This reality is a mark of the new paradigm. The challenge it presents, however, involves the very integrity of the mission of the Episcopal Church. Unless every congregation, no matter how small or how large, reflects in some way a living connection with the larger, global church, the message that we are called to be "members one of another" will be diminished. The building of connections—small churches with large churches, urban churches with suburban churches, churches in the United States with churches in other parts of the world—this is the spirit of mission that defines the emerging church. To respond in faithfulness to what God is surely calling us to do will require not only a renewed global vision, but also new structures and new connections and a new self-understanding based on Jesus the Servant who came amongst us not to *be* served, but to serve.

The New Laity

All Christian denominations are experiencing the emergence of a rapidly expanding group of men and women who have stepped forward to claim their baptismal ministry. The movement to reclaim the ministry of the laity within the life of the church and the world took on a particular intensity in the years just following World War II. The wide-spread response to Hendrick Kraemer's seminal book *A Theology of the Laity,* published in 1958, made it clear that a shift was taking place in the church that would have significant impact on the future. Since Kraemer's classic, the number of books concerned with the recovery of the ministry of all Christians now numbers in the thousands.

In one way or another, every Christian denomination has found ways to reinforce this vision both in worship and program. The publication of the revised 1979 *Book of Common Prayer* in the Episcopal Church placed the liturgy of holy baptism in the center of the Church's corporate worship; a corresponding theology of ministry gave the laity a new sense of their own authority for ministry as baptized servants of Jesus Christ. Ministry in the marketplace took on equal status with the traditional ministries within the institutional church: with this new sense of authority also came a slow but steady shift in the balance of power. To my knowledge, all churches that have been shaped by the Reformation consider themselves to be churches "of the people," affirming that clergy and laity share ministry—the authority and power given for ministry, though different, to be shared equally. But as we all know, this has rarely been the case.

The clergy, by their very prominence in the institutional church, exercise power and influence far beyond their numbers. What we are seeing, however, is a shift in the power structures of the church that touches every aspect of the church's life. It is not that there has not always been at various times a strong conservative witness or a strong liberal witness among the laity of the church. What we are seeing is a level of disagreement that is being heard and taken very seriously.

As in all change, this shift provides cause for celebration and for concern. The recovery of the ministry of the laity is a recovery of the fullness of the church. This is to be celebrated. But the recovery of a strong laity that has embraced the authority of its baptism without the discipline and commitment that baptism requires is a matter of concern. It is the same problem that emerges when clergy claim the authority of their office without the vocation to servanthood that goes with it. In both cases we have a built-in invitation to a misuse of power that can be immensely destructive.

Any congregation of Christians is made up of people at many different places. There are men and women who over the years have embraced the Gospel at ever-deepening levels and found it to be the source of meaning for their lives. Others are struggling through personal issues and trying to find that connection with the church that will bring them the inner strength they are searching for. Some have moved in and out of active church participation depending on the intensity of other commitments in their lives. I shall always remember an active member of a congregation I served who began attending the eight o'clock service after years as a mainstay at the "main" Sunday service. He told me quite honestly that he was worn out by his church commitments and needed spiritual nourishment that was less intense and more reflective. I understood this, having experienced the same feelings myself. My conversation with this man, who had been a great support to me in my ministry, made me realize what a constantly changing scene a congregation is. A strong parish finds ways to honor this varied group, meeting people where they are, as they search for a deeper relationship to God.

I like to think of a congregation as a gathering of people with many points of connection with the church. Some have made the spiritual passage from what might be described as a consumer orientation to a participant orientation, from a connection based on "going to church" to one based primarily on "being the church." These are the people who have at some deep level embraced the gift of discipleship that baptism promises. Sometimes their nourishment comes from deep involvement in the congregation, sometimes from involvements with Christians in other settings. Whatever the context, they express their faith in the way they reach out to others. Their ministry of discipleship is rooted in prayer and study and sustained by a clear sense of ministry both in the church and in the workplace. By consciously living the life in Christ, however the forms and intensity of ministry might vary, discipleship deepens with experience and age. This ministry of Christian discipleship is the center of the church's witness.

Every congregation also includes those who have made a deep commitment to church membership without any significant commitment to the discipleship needed to give membership its focus and grounding. Certainly for most laypeople, church membership is a significant step toward discipleship; they look to the church as a place of challenge and growth. When they don't experience this challenge, they go elsewhere or no place at all.

For still others, membership is primarily a matter of belonging—of feeling connected to an institution that stands for something they believe to be both important for themselves and for children and the world. When one's point of connection is primarily at the level of belonging to an institution, one can be heavily involved without taking the time to ask deeper questions presented by the Gospel. Laity who participate in the church at this level often find themselves overly dependent on clergy whom they like or in competition with them over issues of control, issues often aggravated by the clergy's own defensiveness. Underlying this all-too-common scenario is the model of power seen in unenlightened business. Clergy are hired as managers or CEOs and measured by their success in building up the institution according to the expectations of those who have set the agenda. In contrast, clergy tend to see themselves primarily as teachers and pastors and only secondarily as "managers." This scenario is the basis for most of the conflicts that occur in congregational life. It involves well-meaning people speaking two quite distinct languages that reflect a whole range of differing expectations, usually never articulated until it is too late.

Life in the church must always be an invitation to discipleship. But it must be an invitation to discipleship that takes ministry outside the institutional church as seriously as it takes ministry that assists the clergy in building a stronger congregation. The emerging paradigm is a vision of the church that views the *primary* ministry of laity in the milieu of home, community, and marketplace. If healing is to take place in the world, it will be effected not only by the quality of life in a congregation on a given Sunday, but by the quality of ministry exercised by men and women living out their discipleship in every corner of the world. The emerging agenda for the church is a total rethinking of how ministry is validated; it builds those structures in the life of the church that encourage and support the ministry—in all its forms—of the baptized. For years we have talked at length about the ministry of the laity, but with rare exception little has changed to place the ministry of Christians in society at the center of the church's agenda.

As is well known, no attempt to group people by pre-existing categories acknowledges continually new nuances and changes. Life experiences change us radically. They can cause isolation and pain, or they can be the source of new life in the Spirit. The task of ministry is to meet people where they are in all of their complexity and then to invite them into discipleship with all of its many-splendored variety. This is the meaning and power of life in Christ made possible in the Christian community.

The Centrality of the Small-Group Experience

It should come as no surprise: For more and more people, the importance of the church in their lives is measured through the lens of the
small-group experience. Although still resisted in some quarters, and
thoughtfully questioned in others, the small-group experience is clearly
a mark of the new paradigm in our understanding of the church. In his
new and fascinating study of the rise of the small-group movement in
American society, Robert Wuthnow provides information that I found
rather startling. His book *Sharing the Journey* is in many ways a sequel
to his *Christianity in the Twenty-First Century*, in that it seeks to look
more deeply at the meaning of community as now understood. He
writes:

> Four out of every ten Americans belong to a small group that meets
> regularly and provides caring and support for its members. These
> are not simply informal gatherings of neighbors and friends, but
> organized groups: Sunday school classes, Bible study groups, Al-
> coholics Anonymous and other twelve-step groups, youth groups
> and singles groups, book discussion clubs, sports and hobby groups,
> and political or civic groups. Those who have joined these groups
> testify that their lives have been deeply enriched by the experience
> .... Many say their identity has been changed as a result of ex-
> tended involvement in their group. In fact, the majority have been
> attending their groups over an extended period of time, often for as
> long as five years, and nearly all attend faithfully, usually at least
> once a week.[9]

This rapidly expanding small-group movement in American society
presents a particular challenge to the church. Although some commentators suggest that the small-group movement is a protest against organized
religion, Wuthnow's study reveals just the opposite. In large part, the
small-group movement is growing precisely because the churches and
synagogues sponsor them and recruit people to join. The challenge then
for the church has to do with its commitment to the quality and truthful-
ness of what goes on.

On the positive side, most people who are serious about their faith
have had some small-group experience that provided them opportunity to

reflect on their spiritual journey in a way that allowed their experience of God to be deeply personal and related to their everyday life. In a group that meets often or long enough for members to know and talk freely with one another, one's own religious experience is re-enforced by the experience of others. It's immaterial whether this takes place at a Cursillo weekend or in a Bible study group or in a personal journey group; the personal exchange has become a critical element in the movement from being a church member to being a disciple in the life of the church.

In a small parish the entire congregation can provide the context for small-group experience, if planned and structured with care. Indeed, the possibility of such intimacy and trust (not, however, easily achieved) is what makes a small congregation attractive to so many people. Conversely, strong and growing larger congregations are built on the involvement of people in many and varied groups that provide a context for deepening discipleship.

The small-group movement, however, in the church or in the larger society, is not without real danger. Since the small group tends to focus on personal experience, the experience itself can become the limit of one's vision. Speaking of such a group, Wuthnow again comments:

> All too often it serves more to comfort people—allowing them to feel better about things as they are and helping them to be happy—than to challenge them to move significantly beyond their present situation, especially if such movement involves sacrifices or discomforts.[10]

We can believe ourselves to be caring people because we are able to reach out to others in a group, while ignoring those in need in other areas of our lives. Small-group experience in its emphasis on the personal can all too readily trivialize the great truths of the Christian faith or make our own experience of the truth the standard by which we judge others.

A final comment from Wuthnow's important study presents clearly the challenge the church faces.

> The [small-group] movement stands at an important crossroads in its history, a turning point requiring it to choose which of two directions it will go. It can continue on its present course. Or it can

attempt to move to a higher level of interpersonal and spiritual quality. Given its success over the past two decades, it can easily maintain the same course. It can draw millions of participants by making them feel good about themselves and by encouraging them to develop a domesticated, pragmatic form of spirituality.... The other option will require it to focus less on numerical success and more on the quality of its offerings. Beside comforting its members, the movement may find itself challenging them at deeper levels—to make more serious commitments to others who are in need, to serve the wider community, and to stand in worshipful, obedient awe of the sacred itself.[11]

Scriptural Authority and Interpretation

At the heart of the paradigm shift slowly taking place in the church, there is a renewed response to the authority and centrality of scripture that has touched the lives of more people than we can imagine. Time set apart for reflective Bible study at meetings, in groups, and alone has become commonplace in the life of the church. I am still moved by the numbers of people I have seen on the subways of New York using ride-time to study the scriptures. These are not unusual people or people waiting to evangelize me as soon as I look their way, but people who have experienced the Word of God in their lives and are thirsty for more.

To see the world through the eyes of scripture is to see the world in a particular way. When more and more people are looking at the world through the same spiritual lens, this way of seeing becomes part of the paradigm itself. This way of seeing affects the way we view other people and relate to them. It affects the way we understand the world: our acknowledgment of the reality of sin in all aspects of human life along with the power of hope.

The world as seen through scripture is interconnected, affirming what we read in Colossians 1:17, that in Christ "all things hold together." And it is through scripture, empowered by faith, that we see the risen Christ present in the world and in our lives through the Holy Spirit. This, and much, much more, is what familiarity with the scriptures can mean.

But as we all know, for the church the scriptures can be as much a source of division as of unity. The holy scriptures are not as yet a central element in the emerging but not fully evolved paradigm. In this context, the power of the authority of scripture lies not only in what they tell us about the past and the present, but also in what they point to in the future.

The recovery of the Bible as a source of authority in people's lives is a sign of both promise and pain. The scriptures are an embodiment of the hope that is the fruit of our faith. But, we sadly confess, they are also the major source of the disunity that keeps Christians at arm's length from one another and often at arm's length from other members of the human family as well. Once we move beyond our common affirmation of the great doctrinal truths of scripture (the Creation, our redemption through the death and resurrection of Jesus Christ, and our sanctification through the work of the Spirit) and ask what in fact this means, we begin to interpret what we have been given from many different perspectives— the intensity of disagreement being strong enough to produce hundreds of separate groups that affirm *only their* way of seeing as the fullness of God's truth.

I have had to learn the hard way that to argue with a fellow Christian of the fundamentalist tradition is a hopeless enterprise. Although both believing Christians, we are like two ships passing through the night. We see the scriptures through different glasses.

And within my own tradition, and more particularly within the Episcopal Church, some give more weight to what I would call a textual interpretation of scripture (asking, how do these texts provide for us an authority around which we can organize our lives?) and others give more weight to a more thematic interpretation (asking, what consistent themes in scripture most reveal the meaning of God's action in human history and what does this demand of us in response?).

The intensity of the debate over what is biblical truth suggests that the Spirit might be pushing the church again to find common ground. Responding to this push, however, is more than proving who indeed is right; it calls us to ask what new truth the Spirit will bring forth from scripture that will lead us beyond our present blindness to a new vision of who God would have us be. We are being asked to embrace the Word of God not solely as God's answer, but as a Companion in the Spirit, who will walk with us even where we might not wish to go (see John 21:18). In this way we don't need to deny the integrity of what now shapes our belief; rather, in faith, we can allow ourselves to be embraced by the paradigm before us, trusting that the Spirit will show us afresh what Paul saw as the better way, described in 1 Corinthians 13.

Eugene Peterson, in his book *The Contemplative Pastor,* comments at some length about the vision that the essayist, novelist, and poet Annie Dillard brings to our world. One paragraph in particular struck me as a new paradigm statement in reference to the interpretation of scripture.

She has assimilated Scripture so thoroughly, so saturated with its cadences and images, that it is simply at hand, unbidden, as context and metaphor for whatever she happens to be writing about. She does not, though, use Scripture to prove or document; it is not a truth she uses but one she lives. Her knowledge of Scripture is stored in her right brain rather than her left; nourishment for the praying imagination rather than fuel for apologetic argument.[12]

Leadership for a New Paradigm

In one way or another, this entire book is about leadership in the new paradigm. Its focus is on the clergy of the Episcopal Church as one point of entry into a particular system. As noted in this chapter, forces at work in the church, which in most cases also are reflected in the world around us, raise particular concerns about the kind of leadership we will need. In one way or another, what follows in this book will seek to address these concerns.

In his wise and almost poetic book *Leadership Is an Art,* Max DePree draws on the wisdom of a leader from an earlier time to make clear what is before us.

Justice Oliver Wendell Holmes is reported to have said this about simplicity. "I would not give a fig for the simplicity this side of complexity, but I would give my life for the simplicity on the other side of complexity." To be at the living edge is to search out the "simplicity on the other side of complexity."[13]

There is no greater challenge before the church today.

Leadership
in an Era of Turbulence

In response to Jim Fenhagen's picture of a world divided between those whose black/white, either/or thinking tends to lead to hatred, and the hope of some that we might build a common vision, Davida Crabtree commented, "It made me wonder whether the vocation to which the mainline churches might be called in this era isn't becoming clearer: to serve as a witness to, and lively demonstration of, a quality of openness and dialogue in the midst of a society of increasing polarization. Perhaps if that mission became clearer, it could galvanize us to reclaim that heritage of 'exploration and openness as a doorway to faith' for ourselves in the process. At this point, it looks like mainline denominations are polarizing as much as society!"

The Promise That Is Before Us

The concern expressed above is not news to those of us who have listened to church debates that left us worried about our divisions and discouraged by a church that does seem "more concerned with holding our fingers in the dike than discerning the presence of God in the water." Yet Michael Cooper-White wonders, "Is the church really more dominated by 'institutional concerns' now than in the fifties and sixties?"

Widespread acedia is not news to our responders. Art Gafke notes similarities to his experience in the UMC. "Particularly is there a (mostly unaddressed) fear in the church population and a widespread acedia among clergy (especially white male clergy). Part of the fear is among the aging church population who experience the church as the one 'nonchanging' reality of their lives. These people resist and resent changes in their medium small-sized churches, showing a deeply based fear. There is also fear among parents who want the church to provide aid and reinforcement of the socialization of their children within the cultural boundaries with which the parents are comfortable... The acedia which infects the UMC surfaces around the membership loss and the lack of a convincing vision of the Spirit-filled ministry of a large denomination in a time when membership has dropped."

Davida Crabtree also observes "among many of my colleagues in parish ministry full blown cases of 'acedia.' Their cynicism and loss of hope is accompanied by despair and a strong sense of inadequacy in their vocation." But she goes on to say, "I also observe many who are stimulated and thriving in the new environment. They tend to be persons who take the best of what they know, then push the edges of that knowledge and skill to some level of risk taking in their ministries."

The Emergence of a New Paradigm

Fenhagen suggests several ways to think about the paradigm shift that might serve as "lenses" to help us look at what's happening to clergy today. Here are some responders' comments.

Think Locally, Act Globally

Our main line clergy experts respond to these thoughts in ways that may not surprise us.

Arthur Gafke: "While localism has impacted the UMC with an increasing percentage of money staying at the local level, the positive ministry through conference and general church is still affirmed in many local churches...[But] the strong ministries of local churches, of conferences and general church agencies, of church related institutions have not been affirmed in a unifying way which merges as a commanding vision for the whole denomination. The basic material is present for such unifying affirmation and vision."

Davida Crabtree: "In the United Church of Christ, our sense of authority has always begun on the local level as we have prized the 'autonomy of the local church.' So the shift toward localism has been more subtle for us, and perhaps less historically trackable. However, the shift is just as real. Where once a powerful vision of a national and global mission bound us together, in the post-Christendom era lessening clarity about and commitment to that mission combine with local authority to create a high level of independence."

Mary V. Atkinson: "Polarization in society and in the PCUSA denomination beyond the local congregation seems to be causing people to withdraw to their own locale and to ignore the fights 'out there.' I hear people say that their local congregation is healthy and involved in its own particular mission. This is good news, but for a denomination that is based on a series of interrelated governing bodies, it is not such good news if it means we are becoming more congregational."

Michael Cooper-White: "We Lutherans have always had more widespread ambivalence about matters of authority. The title 'bishop' was only recently adopted; we don't have a separate ordination for them, they're not in office 'for life'; we've never had the sense of global communion which you Anglicans have. We're scratching our heads to determine who would be a 'counterpart' to the Archbishop of Canterbury to represent us in the 1996 joint gathering of the ELCA Conference of Bishops and your House of Bishops. So the experience of 'de-centralization' or diffusion of authority may be less pronounced for us than for you."

The New Laity

Are laity taking new power? If so, is it power for mission or institutional control? Mary V. Atkinson says, "I do see that more and more lay people see themselves as partners in mission with clergy and other church professionals. Of course, the church member who is on the edge of involvement in the church would probably not think in these terms. If clergy are not willing (or maybe unable) to be partners with lay people, then it is less likely that we'll see this 'new laity.' So it seems to depend on clergy's reaching out/letting go, and on lay people wanting to be more completely/meaningfully involved in mission. It appears as though it needs to be a 'both-and,' rather than an 'either-or.'" Davida Crabtree comments, "You have struck a chord with your comments on the new laity, although in my observation the denominations have not by any means caught up with those they seek to lead in this regard. If there has been a power shift in the Episcopal Church, I celebrate that. There has been no parallel power shift in the UCC. However, over the past century, as many laity have surpassed their clergy in education, the traditional teaching authority of the minister has been in decline. This in our denomination has contributed to the level of acedia among the clergy.

"Ironically, the UCC, with its congregational authority, has in fact become quite clergy dominated in its denominational structures and voting patterns. Adding to the irony is the powerlessness the clergy feel. As a church, we need and want a church truly governed by the local congregation. Finding a healthy balance through a healthy process is one of the challenges of this era."

The power balance between clergy and laity seems full of paradox and counterpoint. As I have heard them over the past two decades or so, Episcopalians have placed more emphasis on the ministry of the laity than any other denomination I know. Possibly one stimulus for this has been the traditionally "high" view of clergy authority: here was a balance seeking to be readjusted. Within and beyond the Episcopal Church, however, many of us (laity especially) would wonder with Crabtree how much real shift all the verbiage represents. (At times I feel an overabundance of politically correct statements about lay ministry has the *opposite* effect—one of boring us and lulling us to sleep. See Chapter 5.) An important clue can be seen in the clergy's self-perceived powerlessness. But again, that is the more likely result not of the strong sense of ministry on the part of lay people that would leave their pastors feeling like effective teachers, but of a "we can fire you" posture of control and truculence!

Scriptural Authority and Tradition

How might the Spirit be pushing the church to find common ground and mutual understanding? "At the risk of oversimplifying and perhaps even caricaturing the divisions in our denominations, I have found that I am helped to think about these things by the simple device of the Myers-Briggs Type Indicator," says Davida Crabtree. "It is an insight I gained through my teaching scripture in the local church I served in Connecticut.

To wit: the great majority of our clergy and denominational leaders are almost certainly intuitives, and great numbers of our laity are sensate. Intuitives are energized and gripped by conceptual and global knowing; sensates are energized and gripped by concrete and specific, sequential knowing. As a pastor, and now as a conference minister, I must be sensitive to the 'ways of knowing' around me and make my teaching accessible to all. For those who are sensate, naming the name of Jesus is critically important to their spiritual journey and self-understanding. For those who are intuitive, the great themes of the faith and the other persons of the Trinity may be more the spiritual focus. I have a hunch these differences play themselves out in our denominational divisions when leaders do not pay sufficient attention to the spiritual needs of all the people. This is not an attempt to reduce all the substantive theological ferment to personality differences; simply a device to remind us that we share the journey with others who do not think or know the way we do!" (Note: Those who want to pursue Crabtree's important point may find a helpful resource in *How We Belong, Fight, and Pray: The MBTI as a Key to Congregational Dynamics*, by Lloyd Edwards—an Alban book.)

Summary

Let's close the comments on this chapter with another balancing statement, this time from Michael Cooper-White: "How are things different today in the 'typical' congregation than they were twenty-five years ago? Is there not much in the shattering of some old paradigms which we can celebrate (i.e., women's ordination, better clergy compensation, more focus on ministry 'within the shadow of the steeple,' a less paternalistic understanding of global mission)? And what have been the genuine losses? Where are the opportunities for renewal of the church by following the promptings of the Spirit who, as you say, could just happen to be as or more active in 'the world' as within the church as institution?"

CHAPTER 2

A Profile of Episcopal Clergy

Statistics are not generally fun to read, but they are interesting, and usually informative. To develop a profile of the state of the clergy of the Episcopal Church, I would like to begin with a few numbers that give some quantitative idea of who we are talking about. In 1992 the Episcopal Church in the United States claimed 15,906 clergy ordained to the priesthood, 14,691 men and 1,215 women. In the same year, an additional 1,524 men and women served as ordained deacons throughout the denomination. Out of this total, 8,021 clergy were serving 7,391 congregations. Forecasts indicated that the number of congregations affording a full-time clergyperson would continue to decline while the number of clergy in the church would continue to hold steady. The remaining 7,885 clergy who made up the 1992 total were serving in various situations other than the local congregation.

In 1992 the Episcopal Church reported 2,491,991 baptized members (an increase of .07 percent from 1991). In this same year it reported 1,614,081 confirmed communicants in good standing (a decrease of .04 percent from 1991). In comparison with the other larger denominational bodies with which it is generally associated, the Episcopal Church is small indeed, but, through the grace of God, it continues to be, as one observer put it, "a large house" welcoming the diversity evident in the nation's population, despite the conflict that this quite naturally produces.

An Overview of the State of the Clergy

Over the last six years, the Cornerstone Project has participated in two
major studies that have sought to address the general well-being of
Episcopal clergy; one study was an extension of an earlier larger study.
In 1989 the Episcopal Church Foundation (the parent body of the Cornerstone Project) commissioned Loren Mead of The Alban Institute and
Barry Evans, director of the Grubb Institute, to conduct a study that
would provide the data necessary for the Cornerstone Project to establish
its priorities and direction. The study was small in scope, basing its findings on information received from questionnaires and follow-up interviews.

All in all, twenty bishops were interviewed; in eight dioceses where
bishops were interviewed in person, groups of clergy were also interviewed. The data that emerged from this study contained no real surprises. The majority of the clergy in these eight dioceses felt a strong
sense of satisfaction in their ministries, noting, however, a sense of disconnection from the bishop of the diocese in which they served, some
confusion over what it meant to be ordained at this time in history, and
the lack of a sense of a common mission. As the final report on the study
notes:

> Some of the clergy could understand what it meant to run a religious
> organization and felt that they were doing a pretty good job, but they
> were worried that it was taking over the priestly role and that they
> weren't quite sure anymore what the priestly role was.[1]

The twenty bishops who participated in the study also expressed a
strong sense of overall satisfaction in what they were doing, but acknowledged the frustrations they felt over their inability to reach those clergy
who needed support the most. "How can we turn around the bitching,
the denial, blaming the diocese and themselves?" one bishop commented.
Another said, "How can we help clergy take charge of their own lives?"[2]
Acknowledging that the line between satisfaction and dysfunction was
in many cases thin indeed, it was noted that "the malaise is not going to
be solved by addressing individuals; the system is not working for us."
What is needed is "systems change, mental change."[3]

The second study in which the Cornerstone Project was directly

involved is still in progress. In an effort to get an accurate reading on the
health and well-being of clergy and their families, the Episcopal Family
Network initiated the Clergy Family Project which was able to gather
data from 1,750 clergy and 1,200 spouses from eighteen dioceses across
the country. Building on this study, the Cornerstone Project linked up
with the Clergy Family Project and the Church Pension Fund to expand
this project and establish a method to keep the information current and to
reach a larger segment of the clergy population, both married and not
married. To date, in its pretest stage, this study has involved 222 clergy
and 40 spouses.

Learnings from the Clergy Family Project

In their 1992 Clergy Family Project study, "Healthy Clergy, Wounded
Healers: Their Families and Their Ministries," Dr. Adair Lummis and
Roberta Walmsley report that approximately 30 percent of Episcopal
parochial clergy and 27 percent of their spouses exhibit a high degree of
health and personal satisfaction. On the other end of the scale, 19 percent of the clergy and 28 percent of their spouses rated fair to poor in
their sense of satisfaction and in their general sense of well-being. This
leaves in the middle range 51 percent of Episcopal parochial clergy and
45 percent of clergy spouses whose lives and ministry would be greatly
strengthened and dysfunction prevented by well-thought-out systems of
support.
      In the follow-up study, "The Episcopal Health and Vocational In-
ventory," conducted two years later by the Cornerstone Project, the
Clergy Family Project, and the Church Pension Fund, the percentage of
clergy indicating a high degree of satisfaction in their personal lives and
ministries is higher. The sense of "joy and satisfaction" in ministry and
the sense of feeling "spiritually whole" was consistently over 90 percent
when combining the "usually true" and "somewhat true" responses to the
questions asked. These high percentages were somewhat off-set, however, with consistently higher percentages of clergy indicating their need
for "counseling" (36-42 percent) and their sense of feeling "lonely and
isolated" (37-41 percent). These figures suggest, when combined with
the results of our larger studies, that with many clergy in the large 51
percent middle range, the declared expression of joy and satisfaction is

somewhat ephemeral and capable of very rapidly moving in one direction or the other.

For the 19 percent of the clergy who strongly indicated their need for help, and even more so, the 28 percent of the low-rating polled spouses of clergy, the signs of dysfunction focused in five areas:

- severe depression;
- alcohol and drug addiction;
- anxiety and stress;
- marital discord;
- financial indebtedness.

Although many of the dioceses of the church have made major strides in responding to these problems, the fact remains that clergy who are in trouble are prone not to ask for help, preferring to deal with their pain through denial and isolation. As was pointed out in a study of clergy well-being in the Diocese of Rhode Island, there still exists in the church a competitive environment where asking for help is perceived as an admission of failure. Unfortunately, by the time help is asked for, the priest and his or her family are in serious trouble both personally and professionally.

The solution does not require a system that is able to respond immediately to every expression of pain, but a strong system clear enough about what it can and cannot do, that clergy in trouble will know what is involved in taking care of themselves and those closest to them.

Marks of Health

The clergy contacted in the Clergy Family Project study and its follow-up were both married and single, male and female, and representative of the racial and geographic diversity that exists within the Episcopal Church. Despite the intensity of conflict that has characterized the church over the past decade, it is encouraging to note the strong sense of clergy well-being that is indeed present. The factors identified as significant contributors to health and well-being are, more than anything, marks of maturity:

- consistent quality time with spouse or close friend (if not married);
- the absence of major problems/the ability to deal with major problems;
- the ability to establish clear boundaries between congregational duties and private life as well as appropriate boundaries in interpersonal relationships;
- satisfactory private and social life;
- professional self-concept;
- the ability to live comfortably on one's income. "The key element is not the dollar amount, per se," Roberta Walmsley notes, "but the value of the dollar relative to what it will buy and how this impacts on what others in the community are making";[4]
- regular exercise;
- a good prayer life with a strong correlation between overall health and time given to cultivating the life of prayer.

The importance of these factors is not in their singularity, but in the pattern they present as necessary for personal and family well-being. Some of the qualities these factors point to are innate, but most can be learned. As this chapter will seek to address, what is needed are more available (and affordable) resources for self-care and greater institutional support (sabbatical time, opportunities for self-assessment, ongoing education, and so forth) as well as a climate of expectation in parishes and among clergy themselves that clergy will take responsibility for their own well-being, professional competence, and spiritual growth.

Well, Effective, and Thriving Clergy

In 1992 Rev. James L. Lowery, Jr., director of Enablement, Inc., in Boston initiated a study of what he called "well, effective, and thriving clergy" in an effort to see if there were common factors that made for greater strength—identifiable factors that would be of help in the education and support of all clergy. From the outset, the Cornerstone Project was interested in Lowery's proposal for the simple reason that it sought to focus on strengths rather than dysfunction. In selecting candidates for Lowery's project, a number of well-known leaders both in the Episcopal

Church and in several other denominations were asked to submit the names of clergy who they thought were seen by their peers as exceptional leaders. "An effective leader," the project hypothesized, "is: one who performs well and is productive; one who is healthy; and one who has a good balance between the personal, vocational and occupational selves."[5] The names furnished were screened down to four groups of approximately fifteen persons on a representative basis. With only a few exceptions, all the people contacted were eager to participate. This is what the project learned about "well, effective, and thriving clergy":

1. They have solid spiritual roots and most had positive experiences with the church during their early years. Many described clergy and parents active in church who provided strong role models during their formative years.

2. They are bright and competent people. They are theologically clear and articulate. They have gained practice-related skills which enable them to analyze, plan, and act. They have gained human relation skills which enable them to work well with others.

3. They have chosen ministry—both the ministry in general and the particular ministry in which they are engaged. They approach ministry assertively. They have a sense of worth coupled with competence. They are not idealistic either about the church or the ministry. They are realistic, not cynics.

4. They do not feel trapped in ministry. If for some reason they have had to leave the ministry for a period, they felt confident they could do something else. Many have other skills that they know are "marketable." Some pursued other occupations before entering the priesthood; others have taken a break from the priesthood and pursued other work.

5. All provide for their spiritual formation; they describe well-thought-out spiritual disciplines that nurture them.

6. They maintain programs of physical exercise. None are significantly overweight.

7. They maintain ongoing relationships with significant others and, when necessary, seek therapy to meet their emotional and psychological needs. Several have overcome serious issues (abuse, chemical dependency). But they don't want to play the "whining victim role"—and they don't.

8. They have taken steps to meet their economic needs. Those who

do not receive full salaries as priests have developed other sources of income. None of them sees living on an inadequate income as virtuous.

9. They have solid, healthy, nurturing relationships with others: spouse, partner, friends, colleagues, caring parishioners.

10. They set priorities and limits. Their clear sense of self-worth gives them a strong center out of which to function. They are sensitive but not available to be abused. They know how and when to confront.

11. They pursue interests other than their work "with passion," with joy, with satisfaction, and with a sense of accomplishment. The range is diverse: cooking, sailing, computer programming, embroidery, etc.[6]

What the report does not say, of course, is that the people who make up this composite reflect the same disagreeable characteristics as most people, as well as the same fears and anxieties that in our darker moments touch us all.

But this report does say that there are qualities of leadership that can be learned, if openness to learning is present not as a threat but as one of the exciting challenges that life presents.

In his summary Lowery makes several suggestions as to how these learnings might be put to use.

> There should be some method, usually within the diocese or geographical region for the thrivers to come into contact with each other.... But other than as positive role models to inspire and give some hope, we wonder if the well-thrivers can be of aid to the other two kinds of parish clergy. The dysfunctional need specialist therapy and rehabilitation and also institutional discipline. The great middle of the clergy are noted for not seeking help well, not receiving help well, and not making use of the same with any aggressiveness.[7]

What Lowery is suggesting bears a remarkable resemblance to what the scriptures refer to as "members one of another" (Eph. 4:25 RSV).

Satisfaction as a Spiritual Gift

In these several studies, the term *satisfaction* was noted as a major indicator of well-being. What is implied in this word is more than good feelings or a sense of accomplishment. Whatever good feelings come are the result of doing what deep within ourselves we feel called to do. The novelist-theologian Frederick Buechner touches what seems to me to be at stake. In describing that sense of vocation from which satisfaction comes, he writes: "The place God calls you to is the place where your deep gladness and the world's deep hunger meet."[8] And in talking with numbers of clergy, there is remarkable consistency about where this sense of satisfaction comes from.

The experience of deep satisfaction in the ordained ministry comes, as one forty-eight-year-old man ordained for eighteen years put it, "When I am able to affect people's lives in ways that matter—preaching, teaching, and being with them. It gives me a great sense of satisfaction to know that people allow me to do this." Or in a similar vein, a younger priest, ordained eleven years, commented, "Satisfaction comes from seeing people flourish in their faith. Being part of this process. Also to see a community do this. Those moments when I have been in a situation in which someone sees God acting in their lives—glimpsing a vision of life that they had never seen before."

A female priest, ordained seventeen years, spoke of her sense of satisfaction in somewhat different terms. "I think of the joy of providing the atmosphere through which others can discover their spiritual depth." A male priest echoed: "For me my deepest satisfaction comes in celebrating the Eucharist—the sense of awe and joy of being chosen as the representative of the community to be an outward and visible sign—that which people are sustained and nourished by." Echoing this comes a simple but eloquent statement of faith by a young priest just a few years out of seminary. "My deepest satisfaction comes from the personal relationship I have been given in Jesus Christ and the grace I have been given to share this with others."

And then, in my various conversations either in person or in correspondence, a third theme was expressed. A fifty-four-year-old male priest, ordained twenty-nine years, made this comment: "My deepest satisfactions in ministry come from planning and carrying out something that changes lives or systems." A female priest, slightly older but new to the ordained ministry, expressed the same theme: "Linking the world 'outside' with the world 'inside' with the discipleship of all the baptized through programs, preaching, and persona; one-one interaction."

Satisfaction in ministry comes to different clergy in different ways according to their own uniqueness. But from the many clergy I have spoken with over the past two years, satisfaction comes most deeply through the sacramental and spiritual aspects of ministry; or through interaction with people in those significant moments that touch the very core of life's meaning; or through helping something to happen—from working with others to articulate the Gospel vision and then enlisting them to help carry it out.

These three themes lie at the heart of ordained ministry: the sacramental, the interpersonal, and the developmental. The emphasis differs with the individual, but unless all three are somehow connected, with the opportunity for ministry to be expressed through them, the chances are that, in place of satisfaction, we will know mostly discouragement. And the plain truth is that in many congregations the sacramental-spiritual is often misunderstood and undervalued; the interpersonal is locked into responding to individual need; and the development that produces disciples is resisted because of its threat to already established patterns. Unless the systems that undergird the church's mission can provide support and reinforcement to clergy and lay leaders in dealing constructively with these very real blocks, stress will win out. With concern I take note of the fact that out of the twenty clergy who shared with me their fantasy about what they might be doing in ten years, only a third said they saw themselves responsible for the administration of a parish. For far too many clergy, the stress of congregational life takes a larger toll than the church can afford.

Warning Signs on the Horizon

If the data collected from the 2,500 clergy in our studies is an accurate sample of what is happening with the 15,000 clergy that make up our total population, that 19 percent indicating that they are in serious trouble is not something to ignore. A large number within this group have brought their troubles with them into the ordained ministry and have by and large moved through their ministries on a downward spiral.

For most of the clergy in this situation, the ordained ministry is the worst place for them to be. There is no way a priest can function effectively in a parochial or similar pastoral situation without some capacity to deal openly and honestly with other people. And clergy so deeply bruised that they cannot deal openly and honestly with themselves need not only professional help, but also a work context in which the demands do not exceed their capacity to respond. Rather than assisting the priest to move from one disastrous situation to another, there needs to be a way in which someone in this situation can be helped to leave the ordained ministry without personal and financial diminishment. This systemic issue is of equal importance to our concern for recruitment. There must be structured times in the career of an ordained priest where the possibility of doing something radically different is seen as a viable option.

The Problem of Stress

As many have commented, unless there is some stress in your life, you are as good as dead. Everyday stress is the stuff from which challenge and possibility emerge. Stress becomes a problem only when, because of its intensity or its frequency, it overwhelms our ability to cope. How we deal with stress, therefore, is not only a professional issue, but also a spiritual issue that affects the nature of our relationship to God.

For most clergy, the everyday experience of stress has some recognizable patterns. Here's what I heard from a number of parish clergy:

"Stress is the result of the unbelievable expectations people place on you. Everyone has a different sense of what they want in me, and therefore, are primed to be disappointed."

"Stress comes from the difficulty I find keeping boundaries with people, not letting people down until there is no me left."

"I experience stress when my not meeting people's expectations results in personal criticism, often from people from whom I least expect it." Or a similar comment: "I find it hard to cope with the pain of being misunderstood and becoming the object of unfair gossip and criticism. I'd like to be confronted openly. Projection is tough; being a dart board is awful."

But stress, as we know, is as much institutional as it is personal. It comes, as one priest put it, "from being let down by the people you are counting on." Or another: "All the ego stroking that is required to keep a parish running smoothly. So much time and effort is used in keeping people willing to be involved—effort that so often has so little to do with proclaiming the Gospel and making disciples." Or from "no staff or clergy support system for small isolated parishes. I miss collegiality and being able to talk with a trusted confidant." And on a different note, a rector of a small-town parish comments: "I feel enormous stress trying to keep continuity between the parish and the larger church. Confidence in the larger church has eroded. Bridging the gap is very difficult to live with."

Stress emerges from the intersection of the expectations of others and one's own sense of self—between engagement and detachment. A female priest with a husband and children states the problem quite clearly: "Trying to find a healthy balance of personal, professional, and play time." But as we all know, finding a sense of balance is more than a matter of time management. It involves our inner capacity to set boundaries, and that involves the risk of saying no and not being liked. It involves knowing the difference between someone's projection and a clear and honest confrontation or engagement. Dealing with stress involves becoming clear about who we are and what it is we are called to do. The spiritual answer to stress is the sense of gratitude that accompanies knowing what it really means to live by Grace. For most people this comes only as we face into the darkness that is in ourselves and discover that even this is acceptable to God.

Institutionally based stress is a systemic issue requiring clarity about vision and the parts people must play in carrying out this vision. It requires effort in making sure that clergy and laity are talking the same language and are able to hear differences in perspective. The mutual ministry reviews, or their counterparts, developed by many dioceses are aimed to find greater clarity in congregational life.

Personally based stress, however, is a different matter. Unless we can change the climate within the church that breeds competition and isolation, we will not be able to structure, much less maintain, the support systems that are necessary for effectiveness and a sense of well-being.

Problems within the System

For many clergy in the large middle range between high satisfaction and dysfunction, there exists beneath the surface an often unexpressed reservoir of unease. In The Alban Institute Involuntary Termination Research

Project conducted by Speed Leas (soon to be published), four denominations reported on their experience with "clergy firings." The Episcopal section of this study, funded by the Cornerstone Project, takes note of what is becoming an increasing problem. "With regard to the broad research of all involuntary termination patterns," Leas writes in an initial summary report,

> The jury is still out on how much of an increase there is in involuntary terminations, but it does look as if a trend is emerging. Preliminary indications are that dioceses are experiencing involuntary terminations at a rate of about 1.275 cases per year per 100 congregations. When we did the previous research, the rate was about 1 case per year per 100 congregations. This is a significant increase statistically, but it is not epidemic. It represents about a 27.5 % increase in involuntary terminations. (On this issue we are not finding statistically significant differences between the denominations we have studied.)[9]

Although involuntary terminations have been around for a long time, the balance of power has changed dramatically. Until recent years the idea of a "covenant" described the relationship between a priest and a congregation, which was broken only for the most extreme cause. Today the idea of "contract" predominates; the relationship can be broken essentially when either party is dissatisfied with the other. The role of bishop in these disputes has also changed. In earlier times it was assumed that the bishop would stand with the clergy. Today the bishop normally supports the dissolution of the relationship to bring some stability to a congregation torn apart by conflict.

This has had a noticeable effect on clergy. With the attention being paid in the Episcopal Church to problems of sexual misconduct and the disclosure required by insurance companies, the sense of unease has deepened. Involuntary terminations can be the result of misbehavior on the part of clergy or of unresolved conflict. The effect is the same. What once seemed secure is no longer. And, coupled with increasing discomfort with a deployment system that is lengthy, often arbitrary, and highly competitive, the threat of losing one's job is a serious threat indeed.

Conflict and unease, of course, have two sides. In an early issue of *Cornerstone Reflections* which the Cornerstone Project distributes throughout the Episcopal Church, I wrote an article titled "Congregational Support and the Ministry of the Ordained," to which I received a number of responses. One letter in particular caught my attention. "I am moved by how much your article—unfortunately, the painful side of things—mirrors the dynamics of the church I attend," my correspondent wrote. "There seems to be no trust on either the part of the rector or the vestry or the parish leaders. A small group of us tries hard to be supportive of the rector, hoping that love can create trust and partnership where there is none. However, like most of the parishioners, we experience the rector as being his own worst enemy, of being extremely insecure and controlling, and, in general, as someone who is not having much fun in his ministry."

Inequality and Anger

Unease is not benign. It is generally a warning sign of unresolved anger. As the number of churches able to support full-time clergy continues to decline, the gap between well-paid clergy in relatively secure positions and those in part-time or low-paid ministries widens. The problem is particularly acute with many African American and Hispanic clergy who minister in difficult urban situations with minimal resources and even more minimal recognition.

In August 1994 I received a letter from a priest in a small urban congregation in the Pacific Northwest that ministered to both an Anglo and Hispanic population. What he expressed I have heard over and over again from clergy who in many ways are on the front line of the church's mission. "Doing mission work," he writes, "means a significant amount of effort. Yet, those who are in larger parishes who have significant help from the laity and other volunteers, are generally better funded in program, better compensated, and, insulated in the power structure in ways that vicars are not. . . . Holy Scripture calls us to be 'members one of another.' Funny, it sure doesn't feel that way!"

For the most part, the anger we experience today, both within the church and within society as a whole, is anger at those in power. Unlike the seventies, when the anger of the disenfranchised was openly expressed through sit-ins and marches and witness, the anger of those left out today is largely turned in on themselves. The victims of our explosive drug culture and urban violence are, like the perpetrators of the violence, the poor, and the left out—not the powerful. It is doubtful that stability in society will come until ways are found by which anger can be channeled into those structures that show some promise for change. Given the anger now being expressed through the political system, maybe we are seeing the emergence of new models by which to change problems that have been with us for a long time.

One of the most hopeful groups to emerge within the Episcopal Church in the past few years is a national coalition of small church ministries (both clergy and laity) known as Synagogy. Synagogy is a hopeful sign of what happens when people take responsibility for their own situations; rather than blaming others for their plight, they take steps to do something about it. Synagogy is not primarily a political action group within the local congregation (although it shares these concerns) but a group that gathers to affirm the significance of each other's active ministries. They are, as their published history makes clear, "learners with much to teach; teachers with much to learn."[10] Their witness is made in four critical areas: (1) multicultural understanding; (2) changing diocesan paradigms and decision-making processes; (3) the church's ability to reclaim its prophetic voice when confronting situations like the farm crisis and urban crisis; and (4) a concern that ministry not be located only within church structures.

In August 1993 a conference was held in St. Louis, with the expressed purpose of addressing the need for change. The Shaping Our Future Symposium gathered together well over a thousand people to talk about structural change within the Episcopal Church. Although viewed with suspicion by many, it was, nevertheless, a hint of what is to come. The recommendations made to the denominational general convention got little serious attention, which was unfortunate. As the church moves toward the new century that confronts it, all the energy that moves toward change must be channeled and shaped in the cause of the mission with which the church is entrusted.

Gathering Up Our Assets

Despite the negativity that conflict always brings to the church, there is evidence to suggest that the Episcopal Church, like most other churches in the United States, is beginning the process of restructuring for the future. Although not without problems, the state of the clergy is strong, as the movement toward greater personal accountability and self-care begins to take hold. The presence over the past twenty years of women in the ordained ministry—and now in the episcopate—has made a major contribution toward the humanization of the church. On the whole, it seems, women are better at building trust within congregational life, as their need for center stage seems noticeably less than their male colleagues. The responsibilities many female clergy carry, however, are far greater than many people realize, and their struggles with juggling responsibilities may provide new insight into the need for the clarification of boundaries.

In looking at the state of the clergy in any denomination, it is important to note that the sense of well-being that clergy feel about their ministries is heavily dependent on the quality of their relationships with the laity with whom they serve. The authority of the laity is here to stay, but we are a long way from accepting the full implications of what this means for the church and its mission.

The task before the church is this: to learn how best to gather and strengthen its assets for the mission before it. The nature of the world demands that we respond with the diversity God has given us. In terms of leadership, this diversity is an asset we haven't begun to cultivate. History has shown that strong clergy ("well, effective, and thriving") make for strong laity, and strong laity make for strong clergy. The future demands this kind of mutuality.

A Profile of Episcopal Clergy

With the author's initial prediction that congregations unable to support a priest will increase, Mary V. Atkinson agrees: "PCUSA has fewer and fewer churches able to support a full-time pastor." We at Alban hear this from people in a wide range of denominations. She goes on to say, "Two-thirds of our churches have memberships under 250. It is well nigh impossible for these churches to offer a full-time salary package and pay expenses and have any sort of church program. There is a commitment to paying adequate salaries, which is commendable. But the costs of pensions, social security, and medical coverage rise as the salary rises. Recommendations about options for ministry such as tentmaking (bivocational), shared, or part-time ministers, etc., are difficult for congregations to accept gladly."

An Overview of the State of the Clergy

Fenhagen hears bishops venting their frustration over being unable to help clergy who need it or to "turn around the bitching...the blaming..." Art Gafke sounds a similar note from the United Methodist church: "Over the past fifteen years when greater emphasis on evaluation and supervision of clergy has arisen, concern for dysfunctional clergy has increased. For these clergy and many others, evaluation procedures are experienced as punitive and continuing education is viewed as remedial. Focus shifts from potent ministry to power struggles with dysfunctional clergy seeking to retain their 'right' to appointment and service and demanding justice on the part of denominational officers and procedures.

Recent rulings by the Judicial Council (the United Methodist Church
supreme court) have undergirded the protection of clergy rights in procedures that could result in a change of clergy standing."

Well, Effective, and Thriving Clergy

Two members of our case study group affirmed the need to focus on
strengths, not dysfunction, exemplified by Lowery's study of thriving
clergy. Art Gafke said, "I found affirmative the beginning with healthy
clergy and moving only then to those in trouble." Davida Crabtree
agreed: "Lowery's work on the thrivers is keenly interesting to me.
We have focused too much on those who are dysfunctional or unhappy.
While of course we care for them in their pain, it is very helpful for us to
spend even more time caring for those who are thriving or are at risk. In
my limited experience, the thrivers are more likely to ask for help with
appropriate timing than those at risk or hurting." She notes the importance of "the level of match between pastor and parish. This could well
be an important field for further exploration at least through case studies.
Lowery gives us a useful list of characteristics of thrivers. I'd like to see
a description of the wellness characteristics of the ministry settings and a
list of the marks of a good match."

These two responders hold up the insights from family systems
thinking that have been so important to us at Alban in recent years as
we have been learning from Edwin Friedman and more recently Peter
Steinke. We can spend more energy than we have in responding to the
troubled, thereby failing to give positive support to those who point the
way to faithfulness and effectiveness for us all, and implying that "the
way to get attention around here is to be a problem." Crabtree also
points to the importance of looking at the *whole system*, not just focusing
on one part.

Satisfaction as a Spiritual Gift

Fenhagen sees three themes at the heart of ministry for Episcopal clergy:
the *sacramental*, the *interpersonal*, and the *developmental*. "Not many
UCC clergy are going to name sacramental ministry as a satisfaction

theme," comments Crabtree. "They will name preaching and worship leadership, perhaps. Certainly interpersonal and developmental themes will also be major. For a great many, opportunities to work for justice and mercy, particularly in advocacy roles, will be named as nourishing and fulfilling."

Warning Signs on the Horizon

For those in serious trouble, ministry is not the place to be, and these people need ways to get out with some grace, notes the author. Mary V. Atkinson also sees "the difficulty of clergy being able to lay aside their ordination, or even to be recognized in nonparish ministries. The PCUSA has tried through its constitution to provide categories of ministry, but only parish ministry is really valued. And, too often, taxes and pensions seem to keep someone holding on to the ordained status. We have made strides recently in the gate-keeping role of presbytery. This has grown out of sad experience with ministers whose gifts are not those needed for pastoral ministry. The 'inquiry' stage of candidacy gives both the presbytery and the inquirer the opportunity to withdraw from the process before becoming a candidate."

Again from a systems perspective, Michael Cooper-White wonders, "Does the system somehow need 19 percent who indicate they are in serious trouble? Why do we continue in all denominations to approve marginal candidates? Would an airline tolerate having 19 percent of its pilots make consistently poor and unsafe takeoffs or landings? Of course, I realize it's not that simple when we're talking about people skills and Gospel ministry."

Problems Within the System

Continuing the discussion about ways to help clergy leave parish ministry when appropriate, Art Gafke describes United Methodist efforts to bring that about: "The material in this chapter is quite similar to the clergy situation in the UMC. The two studies which we currently are undertaking look at the clergy exits from local church ministry. The rate of exit within the first five years of one's ordination as Elder is significant.

The clergymen tend to exit ordained ministry. The clergywomen tend to switch from local church pastoral ministry to some other form of ministry. The rates of exit for clergywomen are higher than for men. We are involved in formal research projects to learn more about these exits.

"Also, the Book of Discipline of the UMC does not allow for positive exit from ordained ministry. All forms of exit have negative presumptions. Legislation is being proposed that would offer a positive exit in which God's call out of ordained ministry is affirmed. Few annual Conferences have either budgets or procedures to help in the outplacement of clergy. The prevailing mentality is that ordained ministry is a life-long vocational choice. This is held even when a much larger percentage of entering clergy are mid-life persons."

As in the Episcopal Church, Gafke points out that bishops can "move clergy as a way of responding to conflict in the local church." He points to the following issues as key to hold up for the whole church: "Seeking systems of accountability and support are an urgent matter for many denominations. The church needs help in moving from avoiding or rescuing dysfunctional clergy to calling them to account and suggesting options for ministry. Also there is need to recover the covenantal nature of the pastor/parish relationship, moving it from the contractual basis currently used. Discussion of the competitiveness and isolation of clergy as a significant factor in clergy sexual misconduct is timely. That is, how does the system contribute to misconduct?"

Mary V. Atkinson says the PCUSA "faces an almost alarming number of charges of sexual misconduct on the part of clergy. This certainly is a symptom of dysfunction within persons, churches, and society." (A number of times I've worked with people who are concerned about the extent of clergy sexual misconduct in their own system and who do not know that this painful problem is shared by at least all the denominations I know about.) Arthur Gafke adds: "Further discussion is needed about the current flood of issues having to do with clergy misconduct and the litigation which the church is experiencing. Mostly officers of the church speak of the burden of responding to misconduct. Can we not also explore the dimensions of positive accountability forced on the church through the secular court system? That is, the church may be forced to do things in a manner that by Gospel mandate it should have been doing anyway."

Atkinson also echoes Fenhagen's comment about how hard it is to find a new job, in a "deployment system that is lengthy, often arbitrary, and highly competitive." She reports a study on the PCUSA Call System. "In an indirect way, one could say that the study came about through a malaise. Ministers found it increasingly difficult to receive new calls; churches weren't finding the sorts of ministers they sought. It takes longer and longer to receive a call, longer and longer to find someone to call. However, it remains to be seen whether new ideas will be accepted. The proposal for a new Call System is based on concepts of assessment and professional growth. There is resistance particularly to assessment, and lukewarm response to professional growth."

To the author's points about the shifting power balance between clergy and laity, Michael Cooper-White brings to our case group discussion his gift of raising the other side of the issue: "I wonder about what I read as a rather negative assessment of the apparent (though statistically rather insignificant) increase in involuntary terminations. Is there a positive side to this? Empowered laity who finally will 'just say no' to gross incompetence or unfaithfulness in their clergy? The creation of a climate of safety which allows victims of sexual abuse to come forward and tell their long-buried painful stories and thereby force out of office abusers whose 'indiscretions' were either overlooked or responded to by being moved to another parish? Is the dismantling of a protected, unquestioned clericalism, painful as it is, part of the Spirit's leading in our time? If so, might our despair be not that 19 percent of our clergy are in serious trouble, but that the other 81 percent of us live comfortable lives and carry out ministries that do not threaten the *status quo*?"

Inequality and Anger

Again, three responders see those themes in their own denominations—here UCC, ELCA, and PCUSA.

"There is substantive similarity between the UCC experience and yours. We too see the unease, the involuntary terminations, the conflict and anger. We too see a new move toward clergy collegiality and attention to the balancing of lives." (Crabtree)

"Again, many similarities, particularly in the struggle for women in gaining 'cardinal rectorships' or calls at all. The need for more bivocational clergy who can serve part time in smaller congregations (won't some of those lawyers keep practicing law?!) Yep, a fair amount of anger. As a synod staff person for over a dozen years, I experienced a gradual but continuing increase in "blaming behavior" on the part of frustrated clergy." (Cooper-White)

"As the PCUSA has seen a significant number of women in ordained ministry, the calls for them to pastoral positions appear to be more evident, although it is still not an easy thing for a woman. As for bivocational options, candidates with 'first careers' need to look at tentmaking as the way to use skills from their 'old life,' together with skills learned in their theological training. There is not necessarily widespread acceptance of such a suggestion." (Atkinson)

Gathering Up Our Assets

Again Michael Cooper-White (who is married to an Episcopal priest) affirms the author's positive conclusion: "You end on a rather hopeful note which mirrors my own optimism about the future of your/our clergy. As an outsider close to the Episcopal church in a couple of local areas, I see some real strengths. You seem to be able to do a better job of creative inner city ministry than we do at this juncture."

CHAPTER 3

Rethinking Our Theologies of Ordination

Every branch of the Christian church has a particular theological understanding of what is meant when a woman or man is ordained to leadership in the life of the church. The key word, of course, is *ordination,* which comes from the Latin word *ordo,* which describes not only the way a community is *ordered* or *arranged,* but also the process by which people are incorporated into that *ordered life.* In the Anglican tradition, ordination is understood as a sacramental act of the church by which the person ordained becomes "an outward and visible sign of an inward and spiritual grace" on behalf of the whole church in which he or she is called to serve.

For most of the church's history, there has been relative clarity about what ordination means within the various denominational bodies, both in ways that affirm what is held in common throughout the church and where we differ. Indeed, it is in large part these differing emphases that various denominations give to the meaning of ordination that has distinguished one church body from another, emphasizing how important ordination is seen to be.

Over the years these various theological traditions have remained relatively unchanged, while the actual practice of ministry has changed radically, causing increasing difficulty in linking the tradition with what is actually experienced. In the life and work of many clergy in all Christian denominations (and in other religious traditions as well), there has been a significant increase in what is called "role confusion" (a terribly bland description for a profound spiritual problem), which many studies identify as a major cause of stress for both clergy and congregations alike. Although role confusion is experienced by different people in different ways and with differing degrees of intensity, we can point to factors outside the human psyche that we know contribute to the problem. I see three such factors as having particular importance.

The Recovery of the Authority of Baptismal Ministry

Although we can rejoice in the thousands of laypeople who have discovered a new sense of the ministry given to them in baptism, we must admit that such renewal has not come without a considerable degree of stress. Laity complain over the lack of affirmation they experience from their congregations (and clergy) for ministries they exercise in the workplace and also in the congregation itself. How many laypeople have made calls on the sick only to be told by the recipient that they would rather have a call from the pastor? And more and more laity taking on ministries within the church heightens the sense of competition and loss of control. As one young priest was heard to say, "I am thankful that so many laity in my parish have gotten the message, but it does cause me to wonder, what is it that I can do that they can't?" In the Episcopal Church, the only functions of ministry left to the priest alone are the celebration of the Eucharist and the pronouncement of blessing and absolution, and even these time-honored functions of priesthood are being seriously challenged. Finding meaning and a sense of worth in sharing ministry with others depends on an ability to clarify roles continually and give and receive support. Where this is present, the functions and authority for ministry are constantly changing with more to do than can be done. But when there is not such clarity, no one is sure who they are and what it is they are called to do.

Loss of Status in the Public Realm

Some years ago, while on a speaking tour as a guest of the Anglican Church in Australia, I had an encounter that was an unforgettable lesson in humility. I had just left the office of the Anglican archbishop of Adelaide where, dressed in clerical attire, I had gone to introduce myself. Just as I walked out the door, I was confronted by a large, bearded, and slightly inebriated man who, five inches from my face, told me to take off my collar because what I represented was of no use to anyone. Having gotten this off his chest, he walked away as if nothing had happened. I was a bit overwhelmed by the encounter. What's more, in the innermost regions of my psyche, I was forced to face a question that every once in a while had reared its ugly head: How really important is what I do outside the sheltered world of the church? In a world where the status given to clergy has diminished noticeably, an ordained person must face the let down that comes when the adulation given on one's ordination day stops. Role confusion can be the fruit of the gap between the stories we have grown up with of the beloved and kindly priest who was known by every citizen of the village, and the reality of not being taken seriously by a large segment of the society in which we live. This gap has a greater impact on the psyche than, I suspect, most would care to admit.

The Theological Time Lag

Increasingly in our day, more and more of the traditions associated with ordination seem at odds with who we say we are. During my years as a seminary dean, I participated in many ordinations that seemed more like coronations than a celebration of servant ministry. What these ordinations communicated was a sense of the ordinand as someone being initiated into that specially endowed group called clergy. In the ordination of a priest, the bishop and other priests lay hands on the one being ordained, communicating a sense of separateness that is a powerful force in the shaping of one's identity as a priest. The question we face in adapting to the new paradigm is "What are the symbols and elements of the tradition that preserve the sacramental nature of ordination with its sense of difference but also with a clear sense of what it means to belong to that community of the baptized?"

In the Episcopal Church the ordination of women has posed a new challenge to the use of the term *Father,* as a way of addressing priests. In earlier days this term clearly distinguished those clergy who adhered to the more Catholic emphasis in Anglicanism as opposed to those who rejected this title in the name of the denomination's more evangelical heritage. In recent years, however, the use of the term *Father* has spread rapidly, not unrelated, I suspect, with the decline of the clerical authority that has been going on at the same time. When women were first ordained and serving as priests with male clergy, it was not uncommon for the men to be addressed as Father and the women by their first names. In reaction to this, women priests have begun to adopt the title Mother, but not without some sense of discomfort on the part of the church as a whole.

Titles and forms of address are symbols. They help define those deeper levels of reality that give meaning to what we do and the way we live. The use of the terms *Father* and *Mother* as titles of address are symbols that emphasize the sacramental nature of ordination, symbols we share with Roman Catholic and Orthodox clergy. They also suggest a form of community that resembles a family where the clergy are the parents and the laity are the children. Is this the image of the church that is emerging? Do these symbols of address, with all their connections with a valued tradition within Anglicanism, say what we believe, or do they block the mutuality between clergy and laity that is so necessary for the mission that confronts us? Given the ingrained resistance within the Episcopal Church to the term *Reverend* as a mode of direct address, maybe the use of first names will win out over titles? Maybe the growing relationship between the Episcopal Church and the Evangelical Lutheran Church will help make the term *Pastor* more acceptable? Maybe we will develop radically new ways of speaking to one another that will more fully express who we understand ourselves to be? As we grasp the implications of the emerging church, we can see the incongruity of those symbols and structures that are so familiar as to seem benign; in reality they create gaps that, unless tended to, ultimately cannot be bridged.

Ordination within the Anglican Tradition

The polity of the Episcopal Church reflects that common polity shared with all national churches in communion with the Church of England through the archbishop of Canterbury. This common polity is stated clearly in the "Preface to the Ordination Rights" in *The Book of Common Prayer* and has remained in essence as the Anglican understanding of ordination since it was first stated in the Prayer Book of 1549. In referring to the three orders of ordained ministry at the heart of this polity, the preface states:

> The Holy Scriptures and ancient Christian writers make it clear that
> from the apostles' time, there have been different ministries within

the Church. In particular, since the time of the New Testament, three distinct orders of ordained ministers have been characteristic of Christ's holy catholic Church. First, there is the order of bishops who carry on the apostolic work of leading, supervising, and uniting the Church. Secondly, associated with them are the presbyters, or ordained elders, in subsequent times generally known as priests. Together with the bishops, they take part in the governance of the Church, in carrying out of its missionary and pastoral work, and in the preaching of the Word of God and administering his holy Sacraments. Thirdly, there are deacons who assist bishops and priests in all of this work. It is also a special responsibility of deacons to minister in Christ's name to the poor, the sick, the suffering, and the helpless.[1]

In this chapter I would like to explore the office of deacon and priest in the Episcopal Church, both historically and in terms of the experience of the church today. What has to happen for ordination to be more fully that source of empowerment for the church it was intended to be? We'll similarly explore the office of bishop in chapter 5.

Servanthood and the Diaconate

Although Anglican polity has affirmed the office of deacon as a necessary expression of the full ministry of the church, in reality, the diaconate has been more a stepping stone toward priesthood than an order of ministry in its own right. There have always been people who remained as deacons, as a matter of vocational choice or because for various reasons they did not meet qualifications for ordination to the priesthood. But until recently, these have been the exceptions to the norm. Most clergy in the Episcopal Church are ordained first as a deacon after completing their seminary preparation; then after a year they are ordained to the priesthood.

What has been lost in the process is a clear and unequivocal witness to the symbol of servanthood as a defining metaphor for leadership in the Christian church. In the ordination of a deacon, the bishop says to the ordinand:

> My brother or sister, every Christian is called to follow Jesus Christ,
> serving God the Father through the power of the Holy Spirit. God
> now calls you to a *special ministry of servanthood* directly under
> your bishop. In the name of Jesus Christ, you are to serve all people,
> particularly the poor, the weak, the sick, and the lonely.[2]

Because for so many Episcopal clergy, the diaconate is so temporary,
servanthood as a primary symbol of leadership is more equated with
dependence on the authority of those in power than as being a gift of the
Spirit for the empowerment of others.

The call to servant leadership is at the heart of the renewal of ministry, since there can be no genuine mutuality without it. I believe the recognition of this fact has been a major factor in the rapid growth of the
"vocational diaconate" over the past decade, this being the term sometimes used to describe deacons who are not preparing to be priests.
There are now some 1,500 deacons in the Episcopal Church. These deacons, unlike those moving on to priesthood, are trained locally in specially designed programs with the understanding that the diaconate will
be their life ministry. Most have other jobs in the marketplace, and most
understand their ministry to be primarily community focused, bearing
witness to the ministry of Jesus in the world.

But as we all know, traditions change slowly. According to a recent
report of the North American Association for the Diaconate, the growth
in the diaconate in the Episcopal Church "slowed to a halt" in 1993.
Many deacons were middle-aged when ordained and are retiring; many
have become priests, mainly in small dioceses with "small or poorly run"
diaconate programs. But mainly, the report notes, dioceses are holding
back while evaluating their programs, one hopes with the intent of starting up again.

In an unusual way, the diaconate in the Episcopal Church symbol-
izes the incongruity about ministry that exists in the denomination between what is affirmed in our tradition and what is affirmed in actual
practice. Many concerned Episcopalians would like to see the diaconate
separated from the process that leads to ordination to priesthood, making
it possible for a man or woman to seek the priesthood without being ordained a deacon first. It is only in this way, it is argued, that the diaconate will be affirmed without diminishment as a distinct order in its own
right. Others argue that doing this would diminish the centrality of

servanthood in all orders of ministry, lessening the power of this symbol even more.

It is a mistake to see these questions merely as a matter of internal housekeeping. They are questions that will determine the future shape and mission of the Episcopal Church. I would argue for the strongest diaconate possible so that, as a visible ministry in society, it would serve as a challenging reminder of what the church itself is called to be. This might mean a longer diaconate for those preparing for the priesthood—a diaconate long enough for a man or woman to experience what the call to servanthood is about, with the church doing everything possible to affirm this and make it more visible. Maybe we begin by recognizing those servant ministries already being carried out by the laity, ordination to the diaconate then being a public recognition of those whose gifts are a symbol of empowerment for us all? Maybe we could include in all the ordination liturgies—whether deacon, bishop, or priest—greater symbolic participation by laity and the highly symbolic ritual in which those who are called to lead are called first to wash the feet of those they will serve? As we look to the future, we must do everything possible to rebuild those gaps between tradition and practice, wherever they exist, so that ministry in all of its forms responds both in word and in deed to that cry that has never been diminished, "Sir, we wish to see Jesus" (John 12:21).

The Priesthood in Anglican Tradition

Over the past four years, the Cornerstone Project has sponsored a series of conferences aimed at addressing the gap between a theological understanding of the meaning of ordination and the way clergy describe what they do and why they do it. Several groups of Episcopal priests were recruited to participate in a reflective process that involved three short conferences over a twelve-month period; all were parish priests. During the project they read papers on the theology of priesthood prepared by several well-known theologians.[3] This led to the preparation of participants' own theological statements about the theological basis of their ministry. The group was quite articulate in discussing the papers prepared by the theologians and in describing their own ministries. But, to a person, there was no observable connection between the content of the tradition and their description of its day-to-day practice in their ministry as priests. The therapeutic language of relationships surfaced repeatedly, the language that has permeated the culture: personhood, intimacy, trust, inclusivity, authenticity, being "real," community, and so forth.

In commenting on the project, Barry Evans and Frederic Burnham wrote:

> The single most important learning of the project was that clergy need to recover their theological roots. Many of them have lost touch with theology as a practical discipline; they need to be encouraged to do theology as a conversation between conviction and context, between theory and practice, between tradition and experience.[4]

Theological rootedness is a critical factor in the well-being of clergy and, even more so, in the integrity of the church's witness. As Bishop Stephen Sykes noted in the paper he prepared for the consultation, "The managerial model for running a successful parish requires an adequately theological context if it is to be protected from gross theological distortion."[5] To explore this context further, I turn first to an article, "The Priest in Anglicanism" by J. Robert Wright, which provides an interesting connection through which to engage what is certainly a serious dilemma.

Robert Wright, who teaches at the General Theological Seminary in New York City, offers an interesting theory of development which I found helpful in making sense of what seems to be happening.

> The doctrine of "The Priest in Anglicanism," which underlies all the various lives and ministries of persons who exemplify it . . . has accumulated five different sorts of priesthood, all of which are interrelated in layers one upon another.[6]

At the risk of oversimplifying a very tight and reasoned argument, I would like to summarize Dr. Wright's thesis in the hope that it might provide a helpful connection between the tradition of priesthood and its actual practice in church today. As I listen to clergy describe the stress they experience in ministry, I am more and more convinced that part of that stress lies in the disconnection between the way we understand who we are as ordained people and what it is we actually do.

Five Developmental Layers

For purposes of comparison, Wright identifies the five layers of priesthood by numbers.

The first layer, *the Levitical priesthood* that emerged out of the Old Testament, was, in Wright's words, "charged above all with offering sacrifices to God, to insure the holiness of the nation, as mediators of God's covenant with his people. Such a priest, at least by the time of Christ, was one who stood before God on behalf of the people at the altar of sacrifice."[7]

The second layer, *the priesthood of Christ himself,* is described primarily in the Epistle to the Hebrews. Wright says,

> The priesthood of Christ is totally unique. It is his priesthood, his sacrifice—"one, full, perfect and sufficient," as the Anglican Prayer Book tradition puts it . . . which is at the heart of the Christian Gospel, the good news that he on the cross has done all that cultic sacrifices were unable to do, has reconciled humanity with divinity.[8]

In the development of our theologies of ordination, the third layer, *the priesthood of the church,* has been the subject of most debate. At some length Wright argues that the references in 1 Peter to the church as "a holy priesthood" offering "spiritual sacrifices acceptable to God through Jesus Christ" (1 Peter 2:5) are not references to our participation in the priesthood of Christ as described in Hebrews (layers 1 and 2), but rather an invitation to the church to lead a holy life. These "spiritual sacrifices" (which *The Book of Common Prayer* refers to as "our selves, our souls and bodies") described in 1 Peter 2:9-10 refer to the holy life the entire community of the baptized is called to offer, in Wright's words, "to God in thanksgiving for our justification and in witness to Christ and one another before the world in which we live."[9] This indicates that the order of priesthood that the Anglican Church has held onto from its Catholic heritage is not that which is derived from the third layer, although obviously related to it, but that which has developed through the sacrificial priesthood of layers 1 and 2.

Layer 4, *presbyters,* is that special group of church leaders who came to be authorized or ordained as possessing particular gifts of the Spirit. Layer 4 Wright identifies as one of the strains of the presbyterate as it developed in the early church. "Although our English word, 'priest' in virtually every English translation of the Bible is used to translate the Greek word *hiereus*, which means, 'priest,' our English word 'priest' is derived etymologically *not* from *hiereus* but from the Greek word *presbyteros*."[10] This is why it is not historically accurate to say, as many have, that the Anglican doctrine of priesthood emerges from and is derivative of the priesthood of the whole church.

In layer 5 Wright points to the tradition in which Jesus the High Priest, described in the Epistle to the Hebrews, is merged with the tradition of a presbyterate serving the community of the baptized (layer 3). In this tradition the ordained priest is seen as more than a representative person within the Christian community as would be expressed through layer 2, but also as a symbol of that once-and-for-all-time sacrificial offering of Jesus Christ described in Hebrews. This sacramental nature of priesthood expressed both in Jesus the High Priest and in the leadership of the presbyterate is at the heart of the Anglican tradition of priesthood. But in our day this very tradition is being reinterpreted.

Without in any sense seeking to diminish Wright's schema, I would like to suggest a possible sixth layer. This would affirm Wright's layer 5 but would add the necessity of a stronger sense of mutuality between a distinct sacramental priesthood and the priesthood of the whole church by affirming the gifts of the baptized through which the sacramental presence of Christ is extended. The priest pronounces sacramental absolution in the name of Jesus Christ as a sign to the church of its call to live as forgiving community. In the same way the priest offers sacramental healing in the name of Christ as a sign of what others are called to be and do. Sacramental ministry does not stand alone. It is part and parcel of the community of the baptized.

Sacramental Priesthood and Baptismal Priesthood Seen as One

The sacramental priesthood not only serves the community of faith, but is also dependent on it for its fulfillment. The priest is not "set apart" from the community of faith to serve it, but "set within" the community of faith as one who ministers to and *is* ministered to within a context of shared mutuality and interdependence. This emphasis, I believe, is essential for the recovery of the sacrament of baptism as the source of all ministry in the church. The identity of the priest emerges from a unique strain in the Catholic tradition that parallels that of the priesthood of all the baptized, but which in our day is being re-formed into a new kind of unity based not on hierarchy, but on a vision of mutual servanthood in Christ. The priest is a part of the community of faith as a sacramental person pointing to the priesthood of Jesus Christ. This sacramental presence, however, is confirmed and deepened not by reference to the authority of the tradition, but by the way that tradition is lived out by priest and people together within the community of the baptized.

The Priest as Living Reminder

A friend of mine, an active lay member of the Episcopal Church, commented on his feelings of diminishment while attending a planning meeting for a conference bringing clergy together around some specific shared concerns. As the token layperson at this meeting, he argued for the inclusion of laity at the conference, which seemed to be perceived as a distraction from the direction the meeting was taking. My friend told me that as the session developed, he sensed an attitude of implementing program *for* people, a kind of consumerism attitude, rather than working at ways to share vocation, share leadership, and share experience. The theological images in which priesthood is rooted has a powerful effect on the way leadership is developed. Many clergy are out of touch with those theological images that at one time shaped their identity as priests because these images no longer fit the reality of their experience. Being out of touch, of course, can be expressed in various ways. Using the sacramental role of priesthood as a defense against honest encounter with others, whether it be through authoritarian methods of control or just plain detachment, is not really knowing who we are and not being able to trust the grace that God gives to us.

Since its inception, the Cornerstone Project, under the leadership of Jean Haldane, a member of the Cornerstone board, has continued to sponsor clergy-laity dialogues throughout the Episcopal Church. These have focused on ongoing mutual clarification of expectations and the meaning of the various ministries that exist within the denomination. The results of these conferences, and the many like them in all denominations, provide ample evidence that clear and honest conversation about who we are in Christ and what we are called to do is a fundamental ingredient for the effectiveness of the church's mission.

Everything a congregation does is, for good or bad, an expression of the great drama of redemption in which the priest is a principal participant. This drama, acted out on its most local level in response to the Holy Spirit through liturgy and personal witness and acts of compassion, is the way that the story of our redemption in Jesus Christ is passed on from one generation to another and spread throughout the world. The priest is a principal actor in this drama because through ordination he or she has been called by the church to be the "bearer of the tradition," the one who assumes the responsibility of seeing that the story continues to be told.

I am indebted to Henri Nouwen for holding up the image of the priest as one called by the church to serve as the "Living Reminder" within the community of faith. We can draw upon many images in the tradition to help form our theology or theologies of priesthood, but what is implied in the call to live among other Christians as a living reminder takes us to the very center of the Christian witness. In his book *The Living Reminder,* Nouwen draws on the words of a Jew and a Christian to anchor his image in the long sweep of biblical tradition.

> In both the Old and New Testament "to remember" has a central place. Abraham Joshua Heschel says: "Much of what the Bible demands can be comprised in one word, 'Remember.'" And Nihls Dahl, speaking about early Christianity, says: "The first obligation of the apostle vis-a-vis the community—beyond founding it—is to make the faithful remember what they have received and already know— or should know."[11]

The tradition that carries the Gospel down through history is the medium through which we encounter the Word of God in every generation. This, of course, is what the church is about. The actors in the drama of redemption are the baptized members of the body of Christ, each with a particular part to play. It is the ministry of the priest continually to call the community of faith to the fullness of the Story it incarnates. "Bearing the tradition" means holding in balance the powerful social critique implicit in the Gospel with God's promise of forgiveness and grace. The call to serve the poor or to do battle with injustice is built into the very heart of the prophetic tradition that the Gospel embodies. To live in the community of faith as a living reminder is a call to hold up the Word that challenges and brings us to our knees in repentance, as well as to hold up the Word that comforts and gives birth to hope.

The power of the living reminder as a theological image is that it requires mutuality for its expression. There is no way the story of redemption can be kept fresh and alive without the opportunity to hear about and respond to the action of the Spirit in the lives of those people who make up the community of faith. If the time comes when I am so enamored of my own words that I cannot listen to others, I have lost that which is essential to my identity as a priest. I am no longer "set within" but rather "cut off." In the celebration of the Eucharist the priest acts on behalf of the community of faith as a reminder that, in our common remembering, Christ is made present in our midst. In the Anglican tradition this act of remembering can never be a solitary experience. It requires the priest, who is a reminder of that tradition that transcends the immediate, and the priesthood of the church, who, with the priest, become the community of living memory. At its deepest level, therefore, genuine mutuality in the full ministry of the church is not simply a matter of strategy, but of identity for both the ordained and the laity who share in Christ their common baptismal covenant.

Ministry Seen Through Theological Eyes

Not long ago a friend who is a faithful and effective parish priest made a comment that caught my attention. He had just finished meeting with a group of young people preparing for confirmation. Looking somewhat defeated, he bemoaned the fact that the young people were biblically illiterate. Although they had been related to the church since infancy, had attended Sunday church school, and had grown up in Christian homes, not one could recall a biblical story or biblical image that in any way made connection with his or her life. "It's downright discouraging," my friend said, and he went on to describe the many demands he felt from members of his parish that, although unrealistic, he was trying to respond to as best he could.

From a managerial perspective, those demands needed to be addressed and a community built that was better able to minister to one another. But from a theological perspective, the real priority was not this at all. The real priority was those children who had lost touch with the Story that was the source of their identity in Christ. If I understand myself to have been called by a congregation to live among them as a living reminder, then the biblical illiteracy of those children would have caught my attention with the intensity of a fire alarm. In the case of my friend, this is exactly what happened. His theological vision of who he was called to be was the driving force in reshaping his priorities. There will never be clarity about who does what until the priest is sufficiently rooted in a theology of ordination that is personally gripping enough to make it possible for him or her to discern what in the long term is important and what is not.

This illustration, of course, does not tell the whole story. Many ordained priests in the Episcopal Church (and in all denominations) are not parochial clergy serving full time in congregations. Many are serving on diocesan or denominational staffs, as teachers in seminaries, colleges, and schools, as pastoral counselors and institutional chaplains; many nonstipendiary clergy work in the marketplace. Although the context is different, the issue is the same. Without participation in a faith community where bread is broken and the story of redemption shared, these clergy very rapidly become cut off from their roots. To a large degree these clergy bring a wealth of often-underutilized experience and expertise. The opportunity is ripe for the development of a mentoring system that enables stronger clergy to be of support to others who are isolated and in trouble.

Timothy Sedgewick, in his book *The Making of Ministry*, clearly describes what is at stake:

> In sharing the faith of others, the priest becomes identified with the faith of the community itself. In this sense, the priest becomes a *sign* of the community of faith, a sign of the common offering of their life to God as effected by Jesus Christ. As the priest shares in the life of the larger church under the direction of their bishop, the priest also comes to be a sign of the larger church and its catholicity. The priest signifies the people of God as a priestly people, a people who in the image of Jesus Christ offer and dedicate their lives to God.... In this way, the priest is sacramental: the priest effects what he or she signifies.[12]

A Matter of Faithfulness

Anyone who serves as a priest in a faith community must wrestle with questions of priorities and boundaries. Most of the time these are dealt with out of one's own experience or the shared experience of the community itself. There are times, however, when priority issues mask a deeper and more disturbing question: "Is what I do in ministry worth doing at all?"

A frequent mistake is to seek the answer to this question in the functional side of ministry. Is anything of consequence happening in people's lives? Is the larger community any better off because of the witness of this congregation? Whatever the answers to these questions, they will be incomplete.

The other part of the answer we seek lies in the tradition in which a priest is ordained. What difference does what I do make in God's eyes? And why me, anyway? The answer, of course, lies deep in the tradition from which ordination comes. It has to do with helping people to remember in a way that makes sacred memory a living and present reality.

There is an ancient Hasidic tale told by Elie Wiesel that tells us something about the meaning of faithfulness. It seems that

> when the great Rabbi Israel Baal Shem-tor saw misfortune threatening the Jews it was his custom to go into a certain part of the forest to meditate. There he would light a fire, say a special prayer, and the miracle would be accomplished and the misfortune averted. Later, when his disciple, the celebrated Magid of Mezretch, had occasion for the same reason to intercede with heaven, he would go to the same place in the forest and say, "Master of the Universe, listen! I do not know how to light the fire, but I am still able to say the prayer," and again the miracle would be accomplished. Still later, Rabbi Moshe-Leib of Sasov, in order to save his people once more, would go into the forest and say, "I do not know how to light the fire, I do not know the prayer, but I know the place, and this must be sufficient." It was sufficient, and the miracle was accomplished. Then it fell to Rabbi Israel of Rizhyn to overcome misfortune. Sitting in his armchair, his head in his hands, he spoke to God:

"I am unable to light the fire and I do not know the prayer; I cannot even find the place in the forest. All I can do is tell the story, and this must be sufficient."13

And *it was* sufficient because in keeping alive those stories that alone give life meaning, the human spirit is sustained and ultimately trans-formed into the likeness of God.

As many commentators have noted, we live in a world that has lost touch with its story. The breakdown of community, the loss of those values that make for honesty and civility and faithfulness are signs of a deeper problem—a world of rootless people who have no tradition that inspires compassion and hope. To be entrusted within a community of faith as the "keeper of the flame" is to be trusted with the key to the human heart. Faithfulness is the fruit of gratitude which is where the renewal of ministry always begins.

Ordination as Empowerment for the Life of the Church

Fenhagen begins the chapter by noting the clarity with which the various denominations affirm their several understandings of ordination, and hinting that it is theologies of ordination that "distinguish" one church body from another. Davida Crabtree's comment seems relevant to these ecumenical epilogues: "It does seem to me that the laity are far ahead of the clergy in their ecumenism. We clergy are very committed to our doctrinal differences. It is also the case that UCC clergy have come into our denomination from many others.* At a clergy retreat two years ago, I discovered that of the 37 present, only two had grown up in the de-nomination and one of those was me! All the rest had come to us since their college years from traditions as diverse as Nazarene, Lutheran, African Methodist, Episcopal, and Roman Catholic. Often the doctrinal and ecclesiological commitment of our clergy is even deeper because of their earlier experiences in other traditions. They are drawn to us be-cause of our freedom and our insistence on applying the faith propheti-cally to all of life."

Role Confusion

Fenhagen discusses the problem of role confusion, a major cause of stress, as contributed to by three important factors, under the following three headings:

*True of many denominations

A. The Recovery of the Authority of Baptismal Ministry

The three factors involved in this role confusion, notes Arthur Gafke, "are also present in varying degrees in the UMC... The theological lack of clarity is significant. The expanded roles and recognition of lay ministry in the UMC includes certified and consecrated offices. Fifteen years ago the Diaconal Ministry was created as a permanent lay ministry office. During these years there has been continuing confusion about the relationships between diaconal ministers and clergy. For twelve years the General Conference has commissioned studies and recommendations but has been unable to make decisions on legislation regarding ministerial office: elder, deacon, diaconal, bishops. This extended process within the UMC bespeaks the significant confusion about ordination within the denomination..."

At the same time, "More can be said about clergy from ethnic populations and non-English speaking constituencies and the isolation and competition they experience... In many population groups outside the dominant culture, there is clarity (sometimes rigidity) about the pastoral office. The pressure for the clergy is not so much role confusion as it is the bridging ministry demanded between the population group and persons, leaders, and institutions of the dominant culture."

B. Loss of Status in the Public Realm

Fenhagen talks about the gap between the stories of clergy we grew up with and the reality that clergy today don't find themselves being taken seriously by the society we live in. Members of our case study group note a similar loss of status in their denominations:

"I am intrigued by the 'Loss of Status' section and the new crop of the Pharaohs who know not Joseph. What of this new generation of younger clergy and seminarians for whom the 'stories we have grown up with' are simply unknown?" (Cooper-White)

"In New England, UCC clergy have been through a remarkable loss of status. In colonial days, the governor of Connecticut was elected by the Congregational clergy assembled in their General Association. Today, disestablishment is complete." (Crabtree)

"The loss of status is also true in the PCUSA." (Atkinson)—and, I would add, throughout the denominations I know anything about.

C. The Theological Time Lag

The author describes the separating effect of many symbols (laying on of hands, using parental titles for clergy) and wonders how the symbols can be preserved along with a clear emphasis on our mutual belonging to the community of the baptized. I am reminded of how seldom the Episcopal clergy title "rector" is translated—these days we don't want to be reminded that our clergy leaders are called "rulers"!

While some groups perceive a widening gap between traditions and modern life, "low" churches are reaching to reclaim liturgical practices:

"In the UCC, since the union of the Evangelical and Reformed and the Congregational Christian Churches in 1957, our ecumenical identity has led us to a greater incorporation of liturgical understandings, stoles, vestments, services of healing and so forth, which come to us from other traditions. The Congregational and UCC churches in which I grew up were fairly somber places on Sunday morning, with preachers in black academic robes and organs droning. Today, while our commitment to an educated clergy remains strong, we find as many ordained ministers in albs as in gowns, and almost all wear stoles of many hues. Tomorrow, I believe we will find many in the pulpit without robes if I read the trend correctly. This bears some need for thought about the ultimate impact on clergy identity and authority, and lay-clergy relationships." (Crabtree)

I believe that the high church struggle to integrate tradition and current issues and the low church reaching to reclaim tradition both reflect the same longing for life and symbol in lively conversation. Says Mary V. Atkinson, "The controversy arising out of the 1993 Re-imagining Conference has led to a call for more emphasis on understanding Reformed theology. Whether the bitterness that seems to exist between evangelicals and those who think differently can be resolved by this return to theological roots remains to be seen."

Servanthood and the Diaconate

As they seek living traditions between tradition and practice, many
churches find the deacon's role a particular challenge:

"Of particular help to us ELCA-ers is the section on deacons—we
now say we will prepare them, but to do what? We're not sure! I take
some comfort in recent conversations with some of your deacons who
assure me the question remains in the Episcopal church as well!"
(Cooper-White)

And in the PCUSA: "The Ordination Study is endeavoring to re-
capture the office of deacon as one of service and compassion. The
office presently is very minimally used, with many churches no longer
having deacons. However, it is not nor would it be an office which
would be a step toward becoming an ordained minister of the word."
(Atkinson)

The Priesthood in Anglican Tradition

The discussion about tradition and today's experience continues:

"Some years ago I read Holifield's *History of Pastoral Care in
America* in which the author leads the reader through the many images
of pastoral leadership, from the cure of souls through scholar to therapeutic models of the present. I believe part of the role confusion clergy are
dealing with these days is inherent in that social history of the role. We
have continued to add to our understanding by accretion. But we have
never left any of the earlier ones behind. The further back in history we
go, the clearer the role of the clergy.

"Within the UCC, we have an ongoing debate about whether ordination is functional or ontological. Most of us probably tilt toward a functional understanding, yet with a profound awareness of the power of the
Holy Spirit to transform us as God has need. Our clergy, like yours,
would do well to 'recover their theological roots.'" (Crabtree)

"The history of ordination within the Methodist tradition arises from
the Anglican Church, but develops distinctly. The methodist movement
was essentially a lay movement within the Anglican Church. Ordination
began in response to a practical need at the time this nation was forming
and there was a dearth of Anglican priests during and following the

revolutionary war. Into that void the Methodist Episcopal Church was placed and ordination was begun by John Wesley, an Anglican priest. However, the confusion about ordination is as prevalent within the UMC as you indicate that it is in the Episcopal Church." (Gafke)

"I am struck in this chapter by how 'traditional' a view is presented by one who speaks of new paradigms! Do new paradigms for ministry mean only surface, cosmetic changes? Subtle leadership 'style' changes (becoming more cooperative vs. autocratic, e.g.)? Or, again, are larger systemic questions the more critical? Are you really calling for new paradigms or for the recovery of and return to some rather traditional understandings that may have been lost to some degree in the 'professionalization' of ministry?" (Cooper-White)

New paradigms and tradition are not contradictory, as I see it, but many of us seem to be increasingly convinced that the way we do theology needs to be different in order to fruitfully pursue the conversation between symbol and contemporary experience that seems to be so important to us in this discussion. We will need theology that is less an intellectual left-brain exercise, less abstract and deductive, more wholistic —more embracing of all of us, all we experience, all those radiant glimpses of the holy that defy logical analysis.

This seems related to Fenhagen's point that the priest is not set apart, but set within. Davida Crabtree explores this question in UCC experience "In our denomination we usually speak of ordination as an act whereby some are 'set apart' from the rest. In my view, this has been quite accurate and reflects what in fact has taken place. My own personal preference is to understand baptism as the occasion in which all Christians are set apart from the ways of the world and given a distinctive identity and vocation. Then we can see that the ordained are those who are set 'in the midst' of the baptized as 'pastors and teachers to equip the saints for the work of ministry.' This is not official UCC teaching, yet it is very much in keeping with our polity and ecclesiology. I am struck by the similarity of your 'set within' and my 'set in the midst'!" My own studies keep surfacing the tendency of women to see themselves as set in the midst of those with whom they minister. So here is another movement toward wholeness, as we join the more set-apart assumptions of men with the set-in-the-center posture women are bringing to the church. Gafke sees this in United Methodism, with its strong efforts to include women in its leadership: "Much more can be explored regarding the gift of cooperative ministry which clergywomen generally bring to pastoral ministry."

The Priest as Living Reminder

This image of ministry, as Jim Fenhagen points out, requires mutuality and helps bring it about. Might this not be called "*re-membering*"? Art Gafke, too, finds the role of ordained minister as "living reminder" a "stimulating image. The priesthood as living reminder would take some different shades for United Methodists because the denomination is significantly lower church than the Episcopal Church. The germ of the image still holds for the pastor to serve to bring into the current situation the sacred history, and to point beyond the foreseeable future in hope."

Ministry Seen Through Theological Eyes

Fenhagen carries the "re-membering" theme into an exploration of how parochial and nonparochial clergy might serve one another as mentors. Gafke continues that discussion: "The mentoring systems of which you write have partly been developed denominationally within the UMC. The roles of Supervising Pastor and Counseling Elder are those of mentoring persons who are considering ordained ministry or are newly in pastoral ministry. These roles carry mutual accountability and support. As these roles are practiced and clergy learn the mentoring skills there will be opportunity to expand these functions for the help of clergy who are in crisis. Currently the District Superintendent has responsibility for clergy in crisis as part of the supervisory role. This places the superintendents in the dual role of being denominational authorities and support colleagues. This tension is held partly due to the short term of office mandated in church law for superintendents (6-8 years).

"As in the Episcopal Church so in the UMC there are many clergy serving in ministries other than the local church. These persons offer significant leadership gifts which are not fully used within the local churches or annual conferences. Systems of inclusion for these ordained ministers are overdue."

And Mary V. Atkinson adds, "Non-parish ministries need to be recognized as valid forms of ministry, reaching groups of people not reached by the local church. Too often, non-parish pastors are accused of 'leaving the church.' More appreciation for their particular forms of ministry is definitely needed. This does not mean that it is necessarily easy to determine how truly valid the ministry is, but this is an area that needs to be kept in mind and explored."

The Bishop and the Diocese in a Time of Change: Reconnecting Function and Symbol in the Episcopal Church

Anyone who has moved around the various gatherings that occur frequently in the Episcopal Church has no doubt heard statements something like the following: A bishop (or someone quoting a bishop) reflects almost nostalgically, "I was never more a bishop than the day I was consecrated. There has been a slow sense of something lost ever since."

Or, from a different perspective, a parish priest or other congregational leader is heard to say: "The bishop is a nice person, but he really doesn't have much to do with what goes on in the congregation. Our ministry at Saint Mark's would be the same whether we had a bishop or not."

Barry Evans, director of the Grubb Institute, spends a lot of time working with church systems. He is quite forthright in commenting on what such statements reflect.

> There are signs that belief in the diocese is wavering. While Episcopal clergy may not complain about the diocese, they often admit that it is not important to their ministries. A significant number of parishes have withheld funds from their diocese and/ or national church because they disagreed with positions taken by the staff. More and more, clergy and laity question value received for their "taxes."[1]

Evans describes this phenomena as the gradual decline of the "plausibility" of the bishop and diocese as a significant force in the life of the church as it functions on a grassroots level.

Loren Mead, in his latest book on the future of the church, echoes this concern.

The bad news is what most of you know in your bones. The old system is not working. It is based on organizational assumptions and functions designed for another age and another way of thinking. It is based on sets of loyalties and understandings of authority that do not hold today. What may be worse, the financial underpinnings of the judicatory are threatened almost everywhere, and that threat will not be dealt with adequately by working harder at a no-longer-working system.[2]

Mead's analysis of the problem facing dioceses and judicatories, and the bishops and senior ministers who lead them, is not a hopeful one, and, to my mind, a bit overstated. There are bishops and other leaders who are rethinking the meaning of leadership in our time and who have made imaginative and constructive efforts to connect with the congregations they serve in ways that are systemic and long lasting. Nevertheless, what Evans and Mead (and others) are saying needs to be taken seriously. The problem of the declining influence of judicatory structures is certainly not unique to the Episcopal Church, but the way this relates to the symbolic role of the bishop is. The primary issue as I see it is not structural but theological. It is not that bishops are not doing a good job, or that there are not people at all levels of the church concerned with this issue, but rather that there is increasing confusion in the church as to who bishops are and how it is that they fit into the day-to-day life of the church. For more and more people in the church, the bishop (and the House of Bishops) is a remote figure whose authority as a leader is experienced only on rare occasions, usually having to do with issues of clergy misconduct or conflict.

The Problem

For centuries the symbol that, along with *The Book of Common Prayer*, has most shaped the identity of the Anglican Communion is the centrality of the bishop in the life of the church. In its stubborn insistence on "apostolic succession" as a necessary basis for union with other Christian churches, the Episcopal Church as an integral part of the Anglican Communion has sought to bear witness to a particular expression of the Catholic tradition. What we say, we mean, but this meaning is being eroded by a congregational polity that more and more sees the role of the bishop as functionally irrelevant. For the person in the pew, and for increasing numbers of clergy as well, the symbol the bishop embodies is something remote and to a large extent a reflection of another age. The administrative aspects of the job are clear, but the symbol of the bishop as a source of empowerment for the mission of the church is rapidly growing obscure. For many Episcopalians the bishop is a judicatory executive with an unusual title and even more unusual dress. What we are seeing is an increasing gap between the function that a bishop performs and the symbol that gives this function authority and power.

I am becoming more and more convinced that an underlying reason for the clergy's increasingly evident role confusion—both in relation to the laity and to the bishops in whose dioceses they serve—is that we have sought to develop a theology of the laity and a theology of priesthood largely apart from serious work on our theology of the episcopate. As a result we have separated that which needs to be intimately connected, and this separation has resulted in a tendency to emphasize aspects of the episcopate that are separate from the life of the churches. We speak of the bishop as one who is to "guard the faith, unity, and discipline of the Church" and we speak of the bishop as one called to "share in the leadership of the Church throughout the world."[3] We acknowledge the bishop's responsibility for the "oversight" of the churches, understood by most people as help when there is trouble. What we have not emphasized is the symbolic connection of bishop, priest, deacon, and congregation in a partnership that bears witness to an episcopate that is not separate from congregational life, but an episcopate that expresses that fundamental unity through baptism in which each member of the body, through the gifts they have been given, is a source of empowerment for the others.

This idea of spiritual "partnership" between bishop and congregation has been stated beautifully in a study document titled *The Ministry of Bishops*, authorized by the House of Bishops of the Episcopal Church in 1991. Rather than taking the various monarchial forms of episcopacy that are part of our tradition as a starting point, the study suggests that we look again at the role the earliest bishops of the church played as the "anchor persons" in the church's worship.[4] Although the document seeks to spell out a broad theology of the episcopate, this strong emphasis on sacramental partnership in the life of the local faith community offers a refreshing, too-often-neglected approach to a basic theological assessment of our theology of the episcopate. I was struck by the freshness of such statements as, "The bishop's role grows out of, not apart from, the community"; or "The bishop presides over the sacraments as a member of the assembly of the baptized rather than someone apart from it." This fundamental affirmation, however, has no meaning unless it is experienced not only in cathedrals when the entire diocese gathers, but in every congregation where the entire diocese is spiritually present through the presence of the bishop.

> As first citizen and shepherd of the community, the bishop presided in both the eucharistic and baptismal liturgies. These bishops were the normal expositors of Scripture in the Sunday liturgy, and there also devolved on them the responsibility of expounding the faith.[5]
>
> What emerges from this approach to the ministry of the bishop, is that it is the entire Christian assembly which is the subject of the liturgical action, and that all the various participants, whether lay or ordained, constitute a single celebrating community. The laity are not merely observers of what the clergy perform. The ancient liturgical texts clearly support this view. Not a single prayer in the early sacramentaries of both eastern and western rites has the bishop or priest in the first person singular, but rather always to proclaim the prayers using the "we" of the entire Christian assembly. This suggests that even acting in the role of the head of the assembly, the presider at the Eucharist acts as a member of the assembly rather than in distinction from it.[6]

There is no way that the symbol of episcopacy in our time can become a source of empowerment for congregational life unless it is tied squarely to the experience of the church as a worshipping community in its most local expression. This is where symbol and function connect. We can no longer assume, however, that the sense of "we-ness" that the office embodies is in any sense a given. "We-ness" is something that must be carefully developed and sustained by occasions marked by a level of intimacy and honesty deep enough for trust to emerge. It is my experience that such occasions are painfully rare in the church. Such trust takes courage and time, but we will not recover the symbolic power of the episcopate without it. In a large diocese, a bishop obviously cannot meet with every priest and every congregational leader frequently enough for this kind of trust to emerge. A bishop, however, can create those occasions selectively and with such a visible level of commitment that it becomes clear that the desire of the bishop to be a partner in the mission of every congregation is a priority that is at the center of his or her ministry.

Role Reinforcement Does Not Come Naturally

When the unknown bishop said that "he was most a bishop the day he was consecrated," he touched what many believe to be the heart of the problem. With the gradual loss of authority and power on the local level, there has been, I believe, an understandable tendency for bishops in the Episcopal Church to seek role reinforcement most everywhere but in the parish itself. We have looked for ways to reinforce our traditions of monarchial episcopacy (however democratized) and this has only increased the separation. Without suggesting whether the custom is appropriate for our day, it is interesting to observe that just as the power of the bishop began to decline on the local level, the custom of bishops wearing copes and mitres began to spread. It is also interesting to note that as congregational autonomy has grown, so also has the amount of time bishops spend with other bishops in extra meetings to build collegiality. Without denying the importance of this, I note that for most of the clergy and laity of the church, collegiality among bishops and the pronouncements of the House of Bishops are of far less importance than the need for collegiality between the bishop and congregations. We need to reinforce the teaching office of the bishop, but such teaching can best be done on diocesan and parochial settings that allow the bishop, through whatever ways can be developed, to be a participant in the exploration as well as the interpreter of the tradition.

It probably goes without saying that every new bishop in the Episcopal Church at the time of consecration hopes for a significant relationship with the clergy and the congregations of the diocese. For many if not most, this is the number one priority. But the demands of the "system" as it is now constituted reduces this priority until it too often becomes perfunctory. And then, of course, trust breaks down and the bishop becomes more isolated from the people he or she has been called to serve.

I see many creative attempts to address what many feel is a serious problem, some of which I will note. We will not change our priorities and institutional structures in any systemic way, however, until we begin to take seriously what the episcopacy means in the life of the church and how what it represents can be a source of empowerment rather than a source of complaint.

The relationship between bishop and congregation, however, is a two-way street. As one bishop pointed out to me in a recent conversation, bishops are seen as outsiders and largely irrelevant to the local church because of an increasingly narrow vision of what the local church is and is for. Unfortunately, for many people who participate in the life of the church, the local parish is seen primarily as an institution *for me, and my family, and my friends, and those like us. Therefore,* the reasoning goes, *anyone I don't know well is not really critical to us, and is an outsider.* To the degree that this is true, the recovery of the symbolic power of the bishop as a source of energy for mission involves more than changing the way bishops function. It involves also enlarging what is too often a crippling vision of the church.

To confound the problem, as my friend was quick to point out, clergy tend to look on the bishop primarily as a pastoral symbol. They want him or her to be a support system for them and their needs—accessible, supportive, compassionate, kind, connected, and so on. They all too often do not want the bishop to be visionary or prophetic or a mover and shaker. Reflecting on this reality, my bishop friend continued, "They may say they do, but only if the bishop's vision matches theirs. Many clergy, and hence their congregations with them, do not generally see themselves accountable to anyone outside of themselves, except in very fuzzy, sentimental ways to God."

To build a sense of eucharistic "we-ness" in the life of a diocese requires immense commitment and imagination. It is not simply a matter of rearranging the bishop's calendar. It will require a willingness to do away with every symbol and structure that reinforces separateness rather than partnership. Everyone in a position of leadership knows the meaning of isolation and separateness. This comes with the job and doesn't need reinforcing. What is needed is some balance that pays as much attention to the authority of connectedness as it does to the authority of oversight. I am always reminded of this when I see in the sanctuary of an Episcopal Church a large empty chair—a bishop's chair—reminiscent of a throne. This long outdated symbol has taught its lesson well, and it is not a lesson of partnership. Symbolizing the bishop's presence in the liturgies of baptism and the Eucharist is important, but new symbols are very much needed.

Hopeful "Stirrings" in the System

I was told that a newly elected bishop was asked at a gathering of clergy how they could be supportive of his ministry. The bishop's answer was in itself empowering. "Just tell me the truth," he said. The invitation to "we-ness" was extended. The next step, of course, will be to build the structures that allow this to happen and to see that nothing gets in the way. There will be no change in the way the bishop is seen in the local church until regular, disciplined occasions of spiritual hospitality become a normative experience of who the bishop is and what the bishop is about. The future demands us to place the local congregation at the center of our agenda. The source of the bishop's authority and the point from which all other expressions of episcopacy are empowered and confirmed is in the depth and quality of the relationship of the bishop with the local church. In plain language, we cannot speak with authority if no one cares enough to listen.

Robert Denig, the bishop of Western Massachusetts, who for the past year has been battling bone cancer, says that his episcopal visitations to the congregations of his diocese have become experiences of immense symbolic power. After laying hands on those coming to be confirmed, he asks the newly confirmed to lay their hands on him in response to his request for their ministry of healing to him. As a result of this incredible sacramental witness, Bishop Denig has been able to connect with the congregations in his diocese in ways he had not dreamed possible.

I will always remember a visit made to me by my bishop: I was serving in my first parish, just two years out of seminary. I was involved in and not sure how to handle a conflict situation. I had mentioned this to the bishop at a meeting some weeks before, but nothing further had been said. My parish was a two-hour drive from the bishop's office, and, quite frankly, I wasn't expecting any response. On one weekday afternoon the doorbell rang, and I opened the door to see the bishop standing there on the stoop. He had been in the area and had remembered our very brief conversation. He proceeded to spend an hour with me and then went to see the senior warden of the parish, a visit that began a healing process. I was in a large diocese, and I had no reason to expect such a visit. But it had an immense effect on my ministry. I felt heard, and I felt a sense of partnership that has forever shaped my understanding of what episcopacy is about. I have since that time received a great deal of help from diocesan staff and colleagues, and I have served on a diocesan staff. But that visit was special because of its quality and because of the sacramental relationship it represented. I was not in need of pastoral care but of spiritual wisdom.

The time demands on bishops have changed a lot since then, and clergy now are being called on to find new and imaginative ways to find and sustain what I had experienced. In one diocese the bishop has established a series of events throughout the year in which clergy and laity gather together with him to discuss how parishes can be more effective in raising up the ministries of the baptized. Effective programs and resources are shared among parishes. People from outside the diocese who have something important to share are regularly invited in. The bishop's regular participation has made the meetings effective. He is there and asks others to join with him, and they do. His authority is an expression of the "we-ness" that is being built.

As discussions regarding the theology of the episcopate become more commonplace in the church and as more is written, we will have to look again at the role of suffragan bishops (bishops elected by the diocese to assist the diocesan bishop without the right of automatic succession) and the current trend of assisting bishops, employed by the diocesan bishop without being elected by the diocese. Some argue that it would be better if the rite of confirmation were not limited to the sacramental ministry of the bishop, so that parochial visitations did not focus around confirmation, so that baptism, confirmation, and the Eucharist were seen as the expression of "we-ness" they were intended to be. Other visitations could be made by various representatives of the bishop, including leaders from other parishes with the emphasis being on the wider unity the bishop represents.

I have thought we are saying all the wrong things by having a usually unoccupied, often thronelike bishop's chair in the sanctuary. Why not have the chair (made to match the other chairs in the sanctuary) occupied by a member of another congregation who would offer as the bishop's representative intercessions prepared by the bishop? Why not a visitor from an urban parish to a suburban parish or vice versa? The point is, the chair would no longer be a symbol noting the bishop's absence, but a symbol of the bishop's active involvement in what was going on.

There are discussions regarding giving suffragan bishops geographical oversight (subdividing a diocese), as in the Church of England, to emphasize his or her symbolic rather than administrative role. Such discussions are important because they point to that deeper question of who we understand the bishop to be. Facing this question in the context of today's church will ultimately require some radical changes in the structures of the church and even in the kind of people best suited for the office. As a denomination (and in one way or another, this includes all the churches of Christendom), we are being coaxed by the Spirit to rebuild and renew, not from the top down, but from the ground up where we all stand through the gift of our baptism. The Episcopal Church has for centuries insisted that the diocese is the basic unit of the church. What is clear in today's church is that this can be truly affirmed only when it is affirmed on the most local level. When rooted here, the bishop is able to—and must—challenge, expand, and reinforce the interconnection of the local church with the diocese and with the world.

From Brokenness to "Members One of Another"

In 1991 the Episcopal Church Foundation in response to a request from the Clergy Association of the Diocese of Dallas agreed to fund a major study of the diocese, which by universal agreement was in serious trouble. The study was conducted by Leonora Stephens, a psychiatrist interested in the application of family systems theory to institutional life (with particular reference to the work of Edwin Friedman as described in his book *Generation to Generation*). The study involved a survey of 215 clergy and laypeople and ongoing work with an exploratory group of twelve clergy who met regularly every other week (referred to as the "family of origin group"). This group looked for connections between personal issues and the institutional dysfunction they were experiencing. Several findings from this interesting project are helpful as we consider the role of a bishop in this new paradigm in which the church is moving.

When the study began, the diocese was in the process of electing a new bishop. Historically, the diocese (especially the clergy) had expected the bishop to solve whatever problems arose in diocesan life. The recurring question that emerged when there was conflict was "When is the bishop going to come in here and get this straightened out?"

By the end of the project, the question, reinforced by the fact that a new bishop was not yet elected, had changed: "Well, Dad isn't going to come, not for a while, so we're going to have to deal with one another." It became clear that until the diocese, and particularly the clergy, were willing to take responsibility for their life together—without the bishop's intervention—there would be no continuing movement toward wholeness and health. The role of the bishop was clear. The bishop was not to be the one who "fixed" the problem, but one skilled and secure enough to help establish the structures and systems of support through which a diocese could take responsibility for its own life and the relationships that undergirded and shaped this life. Clergy are notorious for resisting this kind of accountability. The type of episcopal leaders we need can resist the temptation to make things happen by power and prestige and let things happen as people who understand themselves to be a part of the problem.[7]

The Bishop as Servant Leader

The examination of the bishop-elect, part of the liturgy for the ordination of a bishop, includes two statements of enormous importance for the recovery of the symbolic connection between bishop and congregation in the life of the diocese.

> Your heritage is the *faith* of patriarchs, prophets, apostles, and martyrs, and those of every generation who have looked to God in hope. Your *joy* will be to follow him who came, not to be served, but to serve, and to give his life as ransom for many.[8]

It is interesting to note that the heritage of the episcopacy is not linked to power, but to faith; the gift of faith empowers. In the same vein, the joy of leadership is found not in the exercise of power, but in the way we model the servanthood of Jesus. As Max DePree has written in his classic book on leadership, "Hierarchy and equality are not mutually exclusive. Hierarchy provides connections. Equality makes hierarchy responsive and responsible."9 Here, I believe, is the clue to what must happen for leadership in the church to be that source of empowerment and unity so badly needed.

In a recent conversation with a bishop who has had marked success in building a sense of mutuality in his diocese, I asked what he was most seeking to do. "I am trying to test everything we do against the values of servant leadership. My passion around this is that it provides the theology and values by which we can change the institution." Servant leadership is not a fad. It is the fruit of that second conversion that so often eludes us. The form of the servant leader is the only real model for Christian leadership that we have. Yet, down through history, it has been the exception rather than the rule, for it demands a level of mutuality and personal security that runs contrary to our concerns for institutional survival.

The way servant leadership is expressed differs from person to person, but at its heart it invites relationships in which we can "speak the truth in love." Servant leadership holds up a radical idea of power and its use; it requires an often threatening openness to the future. It is patient enough to work for long-term change that cannot be produced overnight; it does not seek to produce change by winning at the expense of another's dignity or sense of worth. Servant leadership is based not on external authority, but on that authority that comes from within as the result of trust and faithfulness. To build this kind of trust within the church takes not only time and effort, but also a willingness to give up the often subtle ways in which we seek to gain power over one another.

If the episcopate is to be recovered as a symbol of empowerment in the life of the congregation and the larger church, we must create the conditions and the structures that allow for trust to build and change to occur. There are many places to begin. The deployment system of clergy is a source of increasing pain in the church involving the bishop in a world of high expectations and little power. This "old" problem continues to grow worse, without much pressure for the systemic change that is badly needed. Any change will require a major shift in our priorities and our increasingly limited resources. Bishops will have to give priority to building empowering structures that connect them with clergy and congregations.

Bishops are elected as servants of the church who, in touching others, also allow themselves to be touched. The world in which we live does not make this an easy task. The systems we have created to empower the church's mission are often themselves the cause of our separation. The authority of the bishop is no longer a given. It must be once again won, not by the words we say, but by rebuilding those structures that do indeed make it possible for people to connect and for the congregation to find that deeper unity that is beyond its own vision and to which the bishop bears witness.

The Bishop and the Diocese in a Time of Change: Reconnecting Function and Symbol in the Episcopal Church

In his introductory section, Jim Fenhagen acknowledges that "the problem of the declining influence of judicatory structures is certainly not unique to the Episcopal Church." Crabtree found "stimulating" "the fact that there are so many similarities to what we are struggling with in a denomination with a very low church understanding of oversight!"

The ELCA, in the midst of *installing* bishops in their system, provides reflections on the case study from that standpoint:

"We Lutherans have probably always had more widespread ambivalence about matters of authority. The title 'bishop' was only recently adopted; we don't have a separate ordination for them, they're not in office 'for life'; we've never had the sense of global communion which you Anglicans have. We're scratching our heads to determine who would be a 'counterpart' to the Archbishop of Canterbury to represent us in the 1996 joint gathering of the ELCA Conference of Bishops and your House of Bishops. My reflection is that you may have some systemic strengths that serve you better than our ELCA approach to episcopacy. I think tenure of bishops is critical. The Center for Parish Development here in Chicago did a major study of Methodist bishops some years ago. Their research indicated that it takes most bishops two to three years in the 'getting acquainted' phase. The last year of a 4-year term is a time when the 'lame duck' syndrome predominates. There may be a 6-month 'window' in the typical bishop's term for creative, strategic leadership! We face similar dynamics in the ELCA, with bishops and their staffs always seeing re-election on the horizon. The other side of this is that re-election is a means by which periodic evaluation and affirmation is given. I wonder how in your system bishops receive helpful feedback

and affirmation. For all its shortcomings, however, I wonder if your
'bishops for life' approach to things doesn't serve you better."

Michael Cooper-White also challenges Mead's conclusion: "Again,
I raise questions about the research behind facile conclusions that 'the
old system is not working.' *Did it really work better at some point in the
past?*"

Mary V. Atkinson links the declining influence with presbytery size:
"The PCUSA was formed with many geographically large presbyteries
and synods. The talk is now of making them smaller—more user friend-
ly. There is also talk about the role of presbytery. The larger the presbytery, the more remote it seems. Its role becomes more managerial
and less pastoral. There appears to be a growing feeling that we've lost
something with the move toward bigger governing bodies. While the
Presbyterian Church does not have bishops, there is often discussion
about whether or not the presbytery is the bishop. The larger, staff-heavy
presbyteries may be less likely to gain acceptance as 'bishop.'"

Role Reinforcement Does Not Come Naturally

Fenhagen describes dynamics that issue in the increasing isolation of
bishops from the people they are there to serve. Art Gafke reflects on the
distance between UMC executives and Methodist clergy and laity:

"The isolation of Episcopal leaders is experienced in the UMC also.
While there is a wide variety of style in the leadership of bishops, the
greatest appreciation among pastors and laity which I have heard is for
those bishops who have a personal connection with the people of the
Annual Conference. There are particular conferences where bishops
have extended themselves in listening and responding to pastors and laity
at the local level. Since coming to my current staff position in the middle of 1994, I have heard comments across the denomination about the
absence of bishops because of general church responsibilities. This absence of a bishop from an annual conference has a double-sided message.
On the one hand, more connection is invited and a sense of isolation is
expressed. On the other hand, the need to have 'a parent' come and
solve the problems is a recurrent theme which allows the local church
leadership and clergy to abdicate responsibility for the holistic ministry
of the annual conference.

"The office of District Superintendent in the UMC is distinct from the Episcopal Church. The superintendent functions organizationally to make the close connection with the pastors and local church leaders and members. In some conferences the superintendents are absorbed in annual conference and general church affairs and are distant from pastors and churches. In these instances there is complaint and problem. In the many instances in which superintendents function in partnership with pastors and local churches this partnership is expressed by a heightened trust and identity of the local church with the annual conference as a whole. Superintendents have been learning that old methods of relationship cannot be assumed to be effective. Trust is a key ingredient in the fabric, and therefore presence with pastors and churches must be developed in worship and other settings that afford this building of trust. At the 1994 training for new superintendents in the denomination the overarching theme of the week was the spiritual leadership role of the superintendent. This marks a significant reclaiming of the spiritual dimensions of the superintending and episcopal offices...

"As a pastor and a superintendent, I experienced the debilitating power blockage that keeps bishops/superintendents and pastors isolated from each other. While the blockage is more than simply personal/professional insecurity on the part of clergy, this is a significant part of the problem. The systems which have failed in adequate sharing of information together with rituals of division add to the problem. For example, it has been my experience that many clergy and local church leaders do not know the process of appointment-making that takes place within the appointive cabinet. They are informed by paper of the formal steps in the process, but generally don't know the in-cabinet process that happens. This isolation stirs distrust and insecurity."

Gafke also contributes an important dimension to Fenhagen's crucial point about the bishop's role in pushing the perception of the church as a place just for "people like us" toward a larger vision. "Not discussed in the manuscript is the dynamic for bishops (and superintendents) who are of cultures and language groups other than the dominant group. These persons carry an important function of bridging that sometimes involves different administrative, liturgical, and pastoral styles. When there is a narrowness on the part of pastors and local church leaders which demands that episcopal leadership fit within a certain cultural framework, there can be an enforced isolation. I personally have witnessed the racism, distrust, and lack of generosity when dominant culture expectations are not met. Also these bishops and superintendents have important linking responsibility among population groups that dominant culture bishops and superintendents do not carry."

Episcopal clergy don't want their bishop to put forth a vision unless it exactly matches theirs, and are resistant to seeing themselves accountable "except in very fuzzy, sentimental ways to God," says Fenhagen. The difficulties Davida Crabtree experiences as a UCC Conference Minister don't sound very different: "The concerns about congregational autonomy, the challenges of building trust, the difficulty of being a visible presence with so many conflicting responsibilities are all very real for Conference Ministers in our communion. You have touched lightly on the role of the bishop in situations of conflict or misconduct. I need to stress that those circumstances are on the increase in every denomination. Ironically, the authority of and trust in the bishop/conference minister are at a low point just at the historical moment when those two elements are most needed for the sake of the church. Building trust among clergy when judicatories are more and more regulatory agencies is difficult in the extreme. Building trust with congregations which see us as representing the clergy guild is likewise difficult. Some of my colleagues told me at my first meeting of the conference ministers, 'You got into this work at the wrong time; it used to be not only fulfilling, but fun. Now it's neither.'"

As I hear it, the lack of fulfillment (or even the killing stress) are exacerbated by personality temperament factors. Many iNtuitive Feeling people go into the ordained ministry, and many of those are chosen as executives by those who want, and hope for, that "accessible, supportive, compassionate, kind, connected" leader Fenhagen describes. But the job to which they have been elected is not the job of a pastor, and in fact a more objective Thinking type can provide sturdy leadership in conflictual situations that tear NFs up inside.

Crabtree points to a way through these difficulties: "The challenges of oversight and guidance are such that we are seeing a marked increase in the vacancy rate in conference minister positions. As long as we allow ourselves to be only crisis intervenors, our ministries will be neither fulfilling nor fun. If we can shift the emphasis of our work from fire fighting to proactive presence and mission engagement, we'll do ourselves and the church a real service."

"In PCUSA, the Executive Presbyter has a difficult time fulfilling two roles in relation to clergy—that of pastor and that of administrator. If the E.P. has to assume a disciplinary role of some kind, the pastoral role is negated. The role of the Executive Presbyter is still relatively new to the denomination, and is still undergoing changes in addition to varying from presbytery to presbytery. Then, aside from a staff position, there is often a we-they struggle going on between the presbytery and the local congregation." (Atkinson)

From Brokenness to "Members One of Another"

Fenhagen closes with a plea that the bishop "resist the temptation to make things happen by power and prestige but let things happen as one who understands himself or herself to be a part of the problem." Following a discussion about how the growing unclarity about a global mission and increasing local autonomy join to make local churches more independent, Crabtree goes on to say this:

"In turn, of course, this means that denominational representatives are often viewed more with suspicion than with welcome. We do not begin at ground zero in building trust, but at -25, at least!

"Unfortunately, this also means that when churches get into trouble and need an authoritative voice in their midst, they don't have one—unless they have overcome their isolation and independence previously and already have a trust relationship with the conference minister or staff. Even then, they are usually not inclined to accept our counsel. Months, even years later, we will hear: 'We should have listened to you!'" I think it was Bill McKinney who said that the executive role that works today is one of *"persistent friend."* I like that: present alongside the other, listening and caring, persistent in telling the truth, exercising authority as one who is avowedly "part of the problem" rather than the power who "makes things happen."

The Bishop as Servant Leader

Art Gafke and Michael Cooper-White found the last part of this chapter most stimulating—the discussion of the servant leader whose authority comes from within as a result of trust:

"This dimension of building a fabric of trust between episcopal leaders, priests, and congregations is the stimulating piece of this chapter. That this trust needs to be embedded theologically and liturgically invites further discussion of how bishops are present: for what occasions, with what symbols and liturgies." (Gafke)

"The most helpful part of the chapter for me is the last part in which you put your toe in the water of what could truly be radical change. It is there you raise (implicitly, not explicitly) the question of the very paradigm of one person, the bishop, being able to function in a job description that every one I have ever known has quickly determined to be an impossible one. I have attempted from time to time to raise up the notion of a 'bishoping team' with one team leader (since I remain tied to the notion that administratively every organization needs someone finally in charge.)"* (Cooper-White)

*Those who want to follow up this idea will be interested in *Total Ministry: Reclaiming the Ministry of All God's People* by Stewart C. Zabriskie, another Once and Future Church Series book whose publication preceded that of the present work. (The Alban Institute, 1995)

CHAPTER 5

The Case for Systemic Change

At various times in history certain words take on almost exaggerated meaning. The word *system* and its companion *systemic* are such words. In recent years we have talked about "family systems" and "business systems" and "political systems" and . . . how many more? But what the word *system* seeks to convey is hardly new. It has deep biblical roots and is fundamental to our understanding of the world as God created it to be. In Colossians 1:17 Paul, referring to the created order, says that "in him [Christ] all things hold together." This, of course, is a "systems" statement. It describes a view of the world in which all things are connected, in which what happens in one part of the "system" affects everything else.

This profound sense of the interrelatedness of life was at the heart of Paul's theological vision, described most eloquently in his great passage on the nature of the church.

> For just as the body is one and has many members, and all the members of the body, though many, are one body, so it is with Christ. . . .
> If one member suffers, all suffer together with it; if one member is honored, all rejoice together with it.
> Now you are the body of Christ, and individually members of it (1 Cor. 12:12, 26-27).

If we follow Paul's thought to its logical conclusion, it becomes clear that there can be no lasting change by simply addressing one part of the system. We need to pay equal attention to those various places where the other interrelated parts connect.

Change Creates Its Own Resistance

A basic principle in systems theory is called "homeostasis"—the tendency within any group or organization or society, as Edwin Friedman puts it, "to strive perpetually, in self-corrective ways, to preserve the organizing principles of its existence."[1] Change creates its own resistance.

Part of the stress we are experiencing in the church and in our society stems from the fact that many of the structures that for generations have shaped our common life are now proving insufficient to deal with the world that confronts us. Bill Clinton was elected president on his promise to bring about what many people felt were needed changes in our national life. The more he talked about change, however, the more resistant the structures became, until most of what was promised became mired in compromise and eventual gridlock. Picking up on what happened, the Republican Party, in 1994 midterm elections for Congress, created a landslide. What they promised was not, for the most part, new programs, but a change in the way business is done—a change, if you will, in the systemic structures that enable ideas to connect. Their promise to "make government work" came as such a relief to enough people that it brought about a radical change in the leadership of Congress. The problem, of course, is that the system will once again reorganize itself to maintain homeostasis, reminding us that no change is simple.

The same frustration and sense of helpless anger that permeates our culture is alive and well in the Episcopal Church. The complaint comes from all parts of the denomination. "The church isn't working," we hear, meaning that what is happening is running contrary to what we believe should happen. And, as in the nation, the first to blame is the president or the presiding bishop or the rector or the vestry, and so it goes. But the issue remains, and it is an important issue indeed. In many areas the church is not working because the structures that shape much of our common life are not flexible enough to help shape the needed change. It is a mistake to hear the cries around the church to reduce the size and expense of the annual general convention, or to reorganize the provinces, as simply expressions of "conservative" negativism. Just as form follows function, so also does structure follow mission.

Some Key Structures That Have Successfully Resisted Change

Edwin Friedman, in a paper that echoes much of what he had to say at the 1993 Shaping our Future symposium in St. Louis, offers some wise, memorable words about structural change. In reflecting on the thirty-three years he has spent in the Washington metropolitan area deeply involved in what he calls "civilization's three major systems of salvation, Politics, Religion, and Psychotherapy," he comments,

> The outstanding characteristic of these three decades, I have come to realize, is the paucity of lasting change. Indeed, I have come away with the notion that most efforts to bring lasting change, by which I mean change that does not merely transform, ultimately fail, and most of the fundamental change that does occur was unintended.[2]

It is difficult to bring about long-term change because in most cases the stakes are so high. What is good for one group is a threat to another. Change in the church, however, faces another problem that seems almost endemic to its nature. We live with an unstated belief that if you say it often enough and with enough conviction, it will happen. But unfortunately, even when our words do indeed result in genuine change, that change is far too often short-lived. Three examples in particular illustrate the point. In all three cases, although there was a change in vision, the lack of sufficient structural change to undergird this vision caused it eventually to fade.

The Affirmation of Ministry in the Marketplace

My first example has to do with the difficulty the church has had giving genuine authority to the laity's ministry outside the confines of the institutional church.

As noted in chapter 1, the years following World War II saw the emergence of a new sense of the power and importance of the laity's witness in the marketplace; the lay academy movement was at its height in Europe, and, to lesser extent, in the United States. These ecumenical academies were established in major cities around the world for the purpose not only of providing theological education for laity in the context of their vocations in the world, but also to provide centers where Christians could gather with people of other faiths (or no faith at all) on behalf of the common good.

Since that time, books dealing with "Monday morning ministries" and ministry in the workplace have had a popular ecumenical following, but little has changed within the churches to reinforce the authority and the critical nature of Christian ministry in the world. The lay academy movement has been reduced to a quiet whisper and the *real* authority in the church is still perceived to be in the hands of the clergy.

Although we still talk about ministry in the marketplace, the ministry of the laity for most people is that which takes place in the parish church on Sunday morning or for the church in the parish house during the week. It is still these ministries that are given primary recognition and authority.

In a very challenging little book titled *The Empowering Church*, Davida Foy Crabtree, a pastor in the United Church of Christ, describes how the congregation she served restructured itself to give greater support to its ministry when scattered during the week. The leadership of the congregation was organized to give equal attention to both church-related ministries and work and community-related ministries. Along with church council committees on ministry in church life and the ministry of stewardship, there were committees on ministry in the marketplace and ministry in the home. It was a simple thing, but it was a clear structural change that sought to reinforce the vision of a congregation that believed itself to be, as we all proclaim, a community of many ministries.[3]

If we believe what we say about the ministry of the baptized, the structures that undergird the life of the church must be shaped to reinforce what we say: who and what we pay attention to in the parish bulletin; who is given authority and how; how ministries are called forth and supported; and how the church structures itself to learn from those who witness in the marketplace and bring their faith to bear on those critical issues that the world presents. The laity can indeed learn much from the clergy, but so too do the clergy have much to learn from the laity. As the motto of Synagogy affirms without apology, and backs up with the kind of organizational structure that makes it happen, the church is a community of "learners with much to teach and teachers with much to learn."

Members One of Another

At the Episcopal Church general convention of 1970, in Houston, Texas, a major structural initiative was taken toward building a system that would contribute to greater effectiveness and well-being among the clergy; changes in the official church canons pertaining to the ordained ministry have had far-reaching impact on the way clergy are selected, educated, deployed, and sustained. As a result of the revision of Title III of the *Constitution and Canons of the Episcopal Church,* diocesan commissions on ministry were established to give closer attention to the ministries of clergy (and, to a lesser extent, the ministries of laity), a denominational deployment office was established, and a movement was started that would ensure ongoing continuing education for every ordained person in the Church. In looking back on these important reforms, it is interesting to note not only what *was* changed, but also what wasn't.

The energy behind these canonical reforms came from a nationwide interest in the greater professionalization of the clergy, the assumption being that if clergy were to receive professional accreditation for much of what they did, they should be held to the same accountability as the other accepted professional groups in American society. To support this vision, professional organizations were established, including the Academy of Parish Clergy and the National Network of Episcopal Clergy Associations, both geared toward developing within the clergy a stronger sense of professional accountability. Also within the Episcopal Church at this time was a high degree of interest in the regular and systematic evaluation of clergy both in terms of their effectiveness and their own sense of personal well-being. And attempts were made to bring greater equality in clergy salaries. The Diocese of Pennsylvania produced a widely circulated proposal that would regulate clergy salaries according to years of experience, the nature of the work being done, as well as the size of the congregation being served. With limits placed on both the low and high end of the scale, there was a genuine attempt to bring greater equality into the system. None of these latter attempts at reform became part of the new canon. Some of the criticism of new proposals was well taken, but much was not. It came down to how much autonomy each part of the system was willing to give up in order to benefit the common good. The problems addressed in these many proposals are still very much with us. The structures we have in place, although certainly an improvement over what had been, don't go far enough to make a lasting difference.

The Myth of Deployment

The reforms of 1970 created in the Episcopal Church the Church Deployment Board and the Church Deployment Office, in order to develop a more effective and equitable system by which clergy are called to serve in the church. The Church Deployment Board and the staff of the Deployment Office in New York have in the past decade made tremendous strides in opening up the calling process and making it more effective. But it doesn't take long to discover that the notion that clergy are actually deployed in the Episcopal Church is a myth.

The Episcopal Church in reality has a congregational polity presided over by bishops; there are very few curbs on the autonomy of a parish. The bishop can recommend a priest to a congregation, but the congregation offers the call. There have been improvements made, but because we have not been able to address effectively the systemic conflict between the authority of the bishop and the authority of the congregation, the same problems continue to recur. When a congregation is falling apart as a result of poor leadership or an obvious mismatch, unless it is a question of serious misbehavior, the bishop has no authority to move the priest until the situation is essentially out of control. Nor does the system as it now stands provide a way by which clergy with particular skills can be put in places where they are most needed, except by a long process that may or may not result in a call.

In November 1990 the denominational board for church deployment published the results of a major study of the deployment system of the Episcopal Church with recommendations for many much needed changes. As with the other studies I have mentioned, a high percentage of clergy stated that they were "content" or "fulfilled" in their ministries. Of this highly satisfied group, however, 93 percent indicated a strong level of frustration with the deployment system as it currently exists. Ninety-two percent of laypeople involved in the search process expressed similar frustration. The study noted a number of problem areas that needed to be addressed. The search for rectors, frequently fifteen to eighteen months, took too long. There was a shared feeling that too many bishops had backed away from responsibility in this area. There was dissatisfaction expressed with the personnel profile used by the Church Deployment Office. And there continues to be a strong perception that the search process as it now exists, as the report states, "inadvertently permits discrimination, especially based on age, gender, race, marital status and sexual orientation."4 For a relatively small number of clergy and congregations, the system works well. But for most, there is more frustration than satisfaction.

It comes as no secret that minority clergy are far too often the group that suffers most from this free-wheeling system of "nondeployment." As has been noted by some, it appears to be easier for a black priest to be elected a bishop than to be called to a "prestigious," predominantly white church. The destructive effect of this critical concern is not only a discouragement, but also the relegation of many gifted clergy to marginal situations where burnout is almost inevitable. Although there are signs of some improvement, the situation continues to be serious. It is no wonder that it is so difficult to recruit minorities to the ordained ministry of the Episcopal Church.

Since the report was released, many of its recommendations have been acted on. But, as later studies of clergy well-being show, the same frustration remains and will continue to remain until the deeper systemic issues are addressed. The continued use of the term *deployment* is a symptom of the problem. The symbol does not match up with the reality.

Taking the New Paradigm Seriously

Like *systemic,* the word *paradigm* seems more like a code word understood by a few, a mystery to most. In simple language, a *paradigm shift* describes the fact that the world is changing in many ways that we can do nothing about. The forces set loose in one era, some toxic, some benign, are the forces that help shape the era that is emerging. One of the most dramatic illustrations of how paradigms shift can be seen in the recent debate over the GATT Treaty (General Agreement on Tariffs and Trade) which passed the U.S. House and Senate in December 1994. The new paradigm is the reality of a global economic order that has been developing for some time. Without arguing about the strengths and weaknesses of the actual treaty, it was clearly a symbol of the different kind of world in which we now live. When 124 nations can agree on anything, you can be sure that, at some level, our perceptions of reality have begun to change.

One of the most intriguing challenges to our way of thinking has come from the world of physics, opening up radically new ways of understanding change, even in the social realm. Out of what generally has been referred to as "chaos theory," a growing body of new social and leadership technology has emerged. Margaret Wheatley, a management consultant and a pioneer in exploring the implications of chaos theory to the world of business, presents this new perspective in the form of a challenge.

> All these years, we have confused control with order. What if we stopped looking for control, and began in earnest the search for order we see everywhere around us in living, dynamic systems? . . . A second sensibility of chaos theory, is that the pursuit of a stable, balanced life of equilibrium is not possible. . . . Systems are most capable of responding to change at the edge of chaos; therefore, if we don't become confident that chaos is a useful state to be in *occasionally*, then we are going to get incremental, small solutions and miss the moments of great creativity.[5]

Secrets, Pathology, and Gridlock

Few people have had any greater impact on the dynamics of congregational life than Rabbi Edwin Friedman, quoted earlier in this chapter. Three Friedman principles of family systems theory seem particularly helpful in looking at structural change.

The most basic principle has to do with how we seek to lessen anxiety by bonding with someone else in a way that makes a third person the problem. We create emotional "triangles" that block communication and create dysfunction. Making someone else the problem prevents me from seeing that the problem is systemic and often within the triangle itself. One way to create triangles is by sharing secrets that give power to those who know the secrets over those who don't. When I think about this concept in the context of church life, I suspect that this is exactly what is going on in our theological battles over who is "orthodox" and who is not. With those who agree with me, I share the secret that I *know* who is out of step, although I have never spoken directly—or listened—to these "out of step" others. This way of relating is a systemic more than a personal problem, and it will not change until those who differ can sit down together and hear directly how and what the other believes. Talking *to* builds trust; talking *about* is destructive.

A second principle and a basic ingredient in any healthy system is Friedman's emphasis on the need to work with strength rather than weakness. We live in a world obsessed with the pathological. Serial killers have become the anti-heroes and their stories are more likely to be seen in the newspaper headlines than the story of someone who has made a life-saving scientific breakthrough. Friedman writes,

> The focus on pathology is like looking at things through a microscope rather than a wide angle lens. Things are seen out of context, and, as one of my colleagues recently said, "in the isolated magnification of a microscope, even a flea can look like a monster."[6]

All we need in the church is one priest to be dismissed for sexual misconduct, and the flea becomes a monster. When I ask bishops in the Episcopal Church where the most stress comes from in their ministries, they almost without exception reply, "dealing with parish and clergy crises." What was intended to be a ministry that helps the church in a broad ecumenical and global context focus on the future, for too many bishops has become a ministry of crisis intervention, which by its very nature places the response to pathology over the reinforcement of strength.

A third emphasis in Friedman's work is what he refers to as "imagination gridlock." Using Ptolemy's theory of the universe as an example, he reminds us that humanity's absolute certainty that the sun, stars, and planets revolved around Earth locked Europe in a worldview that took 1,200 years to change. "Imagination Gridlock," Friedman writes, is the result of "trying to solve old questions with new answers rather than changing the questions being asked." It results, he continues, with "the polarization between extremes . . . so that no one can imagine the infinite range of other possibilities in between."[7]

The church will not be able to respond effectively to the challenge of the emerging world until we can move beyond the fixed positions that divide us and together look for the new questions that we should be asking. We are caught in "imagination gridlock," which could well be the most serious systemic problem we face.

Structure Follows Mission as Form Follows Function

As a young priest serving three small congregations in rural Maryland, I had my first experience of the conflict that can easily arise between structure and mission. These were the years when much of the stimulus for mission came from the national church, where a large and remarkably creative staff worked to make new ideas and useful resources readily available to the denomination at large. As a result, I kept getting material for those members of the parish who had been appointed to oversee a wide spectrum of the church's concern. It was assumed that my congregation would have a world-mission chair and a race-relations chair and a stewardship chair and on and on. Being a young and faithful servant of the denomination, when a new mailing came from national headquarters for a new mission area not yet covered, I appointed a chair. The problem, of course, is that there were not enough people to go around, so we had one person sometimes chairing three committees, some having only one member. Instead of using the resources to support the church's mission, mission was seen as serving the structures.

From its very beginning the aim of the Cornerstone Project was to explore ways in which the structures of the denomination could more readily reinforce the gifts that clergy brought to the denominational mission. A statement by the Cornerstone board in October 1993 expressed its vision of what needed to happen:

> The Christian Church is that community of persons baptized into the ministry of Jesus Christ in order that his ministry might be shared with others both as individuals and through the structures that shape their lives. The structures of the church, therefore, are given as the means by which the ministry of the church is organized and expressed. Just as form follows function, so does structure follow mission, and not the other way around. When mission is bound to structures that no longer serve the purpose for which they were intended, a vacuum is created that creates confusion and blocks the

energy of the Spirit. Such a vacuum exists in the church today and there can be no renewal of ministry, be this the ministry of the clergy or the ministry of the laity, without addressing the structural and systemic issues as well as the issues effecting our personal wholeness and holiness.

Finding Points of Connection

One of the first steps I took when I joined the staff of the Cornerstone Project in 1992 was to convene a gathering of ecumenical leaders in the field of ministry development; most were friends of long standing. The group was presented with a description of the Cornerstone program and requested to give an honest critique of what they saw. Their answer was clear and to the point: We were attempting to do too much with too little; as a result we were dealing more with old answers to old questions than helping to find new answers to the new questions the church was being forced to ask.

At this conference I learned about a program being developed in both the Evangelical Lutheran Church in America and the Presbyterian Church (USA) that, more than any other intervention I had seen, gave real promise for systemic change. Along with the Episcopal Church, the ELCA and the Presbyterian Church had been participants in the study on involuntary termination conducted by Speed Leas and The Alban Institute. One of the major findings of this study was data showing that over 90 percent of clergy "fired" from their churches for problems other than those of a moral nature had experienced trouble in the first year of ministry in these particular parishes. Often the trouble initially appeared to be "minor"; it was not seen as the seed of a deeper problem and went unnoticed until it was too late. In examining the data, William Behrens, of the national ELCA staff, proposed that a program be designed that provided help for both pastors and congregations in their first year together; eventually every pastor in the church could be helped to develop skills that fit his or her need, since ultimately every clergyperson moves at least once. The systemic issue, of course, is how to make such a program normative. In at least one Lutheran synod, a clergy transition program became mandatory.

In the Episcopal Church, such a program is slowly selling itself on a voluntary basis. Working with Loren Mead and Roy Oswald of The Alban Institute, who helped design the ELCA program, five dioceses were brought together to see how such a program could be adapted to local use. In each case the programs varied according to individual need, the constants being two overnight gatherings with all the clergy (and spouses) who had moved in a given year (including the bishop and spouse); a monthly meeting with the clergy for support and disciplined reflection on critical incidents in their ministry setting; and at least one conference on conflict management and role clarification with the lay leaders of the participating parishes.

Since the initial programs in the Dioceses of Missouri, Ohio, and Alabama, other dioceses have become involved as the idea slowly catches on. The question remains: How can such an intervention become normative in the church in a way that builds stronger and more personal relationships among bishops, clergy, and congregations? It also raises the question whether this kind of intervention can become a way of maintaining contact with those clergy who so quickly become isolated from sources of support by building not on their weakness but on their strengths. The long-term impact of this kind of intervention will depend on whether it is seen not as a stop-gap measure, but as permanent structural change that would become a normative part of the ministry experience of every clergyperson and every parish in the denomination.

Problems and Possibilities

Systemic change involves an ongoing willingness to examine the way we live as "members one of another" to identify the points of connection that contribute to the strength and well-being of both the church as an institution and those who share in its life. In the ministry of clergy there are several such points of connection that have the potential for long-term results. A recent Episcopal Church study, *Recruiting for Leadership in Ministry,* provides helpful information and raises the strategic systemic question: Have the structures formerly established to screen applicants for the ordained ministry become structures that screen many potentially strong leaders out?[8]

Certainly when a prospective pastor begins seminary education and then the first year of ministry, the points of connection are many and obvious. The systemic question, however, focuses not so much on the candidates themselves, but on the institutions that prepare them. As it now stands in the Episcopal Church (although there are some exciting signs of change[9]), the eleven official seminaries of the denomination operate independently of the system. They are not participants in the local-level planning with regard to ministry development or ongoing education and training. This tends to create an adversarial relationship moderated only by the loyalty of each seminary's graduates. Therefore when critical discussions take place in the church over the high cost of seminary education or the need for more local education and training of leadership, the seminaries feel threatened because they are essentially out of the loop. Until ways are found to build planning clusters throughout the country that involve all stakeholders in the issue, the structures that have been created to educate and sustain the leadership of the church will continue to be insufficient.

A Time for Self-Assessment

Some time ago there was a cartoon in the *New Yorker* depicting two owls sitting on a tree. The first owl, with a rather distasteful look on his face, says to the other, "You're wise, but you lack tree-smarts." And, of course, this is the problem every leader in the church faces. Wisdom comes from the Gospel tradition, but "tree-smarts" comes from the continual testing of this wisdom in the context of the ever-changing circumstances in which we live and work. The casual approach to life-long learning that exists in most churches is not enough. Personal accountability requires a thought-out personal plan by which every ordained person makes some disciplined commitment to personal growth. Clergy should be held accountable by their bishops and peers for maintaining a plan of ongoing education throughout their careers; this is important not only for the well-being of clergy, but also of the church as a whole.

In 1992 the Cornerstone Project initiated a series of conferences for clergy who had been in parish ministry from three to seven years. The purpose of these conferences? To test the impact of direct assistance at this particular time in a priest's ministry to see whether it had the possibility for long-term results. In short, was this a critical point of entry? We had a particular interest in knowing how in this time period the dream fit the reality; what kind of adjustments had been required?

From reports of and follow-up on more than 150 clergy, it is clear
that this is a time of important transition. As one participant commented:
"In seminary, I seemed to throw out some of my ideas about the authority of clergy; the years since have been (and continue to be) a process of
re-examining that authority in my ministry as a priest and pastor."

Or as another participant, thirty-nine-years-old with four years in the
ordained ministry, put it:

> The ministry is more realistic after living in it for four-plus years.
> It doesn't afford the same position within the community that I had
> expected. Within a parish, conflict is far more present than I had
> expected over all kinds of issues. I experience difficulty with ac-
> countability on the part of the laity in positions of responsibility. I
> recognize the need for an advocate within the parish, particularly in
> issues of dollars. I have found that it is easy to let yourself be used
> and abused.

If we are given the opportunity for reflection and support, our learning continues and the wisdom we have to give others deepens. At a
number of times in ministry, the opportunity for honest self-assessment
may determine whether we stay in the active ministry or seek other ways
to use the gifts God has given us. Honest self-assessment and support
from peers may make retirement a chance for the expression of gifts we
did not know we had.

But if self-assessment is hit or miss, it will continue to be seen by
parishes and clergy as helpful, but not necessary. And this, of course, is
part of the problem.

A Case for Systemic Change

The mission of the Christian church is to proclaim the gospel of salvation
and to live in the world as a visible sign of the healing and reconciling
power of Jesus Christ. Our ability as a church to respond to this mission
is always in tension with the realities of the world in which we live,
which continually demands of us new responses. As we face the twenty-
first century, we do so with declining resources and with increasing
inability to witness to that bond of unity that holds us together.

The challenge facing the church is to move from a system of crisis intervention (which will burn us all out) to crisis prevention. To respond to this challenge we will need to use our limited resources in ways that strengthen normative points of connection without constantly reinventing the wheel. How can we make what works a part of those normal procedures that we can depend on? And how can we build into the system those ongoing sources of healing that make possible the interdependence required by mission? We need those elements of strength that are pliable enough to meet changing demands yet enduring enough to be around in some form tomorrow.

The Case for Systemic Change

Change Creates Its Own Resistance

"Homeostasis is a serious problem during a paradigm shift. Yes, it provides security for those who are anxious. It also ensures that the change that could position the institution to make the transition does not happen. George Parsons, Senior Consultant with The Alban Institute, speaks of our habit of 'misfiling the past in the future.' It's a helpful phrase we can all identify with. The UCC is a freer system on the surface than the more hierarchical denominations. Local churches can experiment and create their own structures and systems, as we did in Colchester around the principle of empowering the laity for ministries in the world. (By the way, two years after my departure, the congregation there voted new bylaws reflecting the structure described in *The Empowering Church*. So it can happen!)

Yet nationally the UCC is restructuring and as it does so it appears to be misfiling the past in the future. Some of the work has been creative and faithful. Yet the bottom line is that the national structure will still carry the same expectations of itself, still be centralized in one place, and still fulfill the low expectations other parts of the denominational system have for it. Yes, that is a triangle. And it is imperative that we remember: it is not the fault of the persons involved. It is systemic, homeostatic, and a good example of imagination gridlock." (Crabtree)

Mary V. Atkinson expresses a related concern: "One regret I want to insert here is that the PCUSA lost its holistic view of ministry with the 1993 restructure of the denominational offices. Where there had been the Church Vocations Ministry Unit and, with the UPCUSA prior to that, the Vocation Agency, the work done on behalf of church professionals is relegated to a smaller program area within the larger sub-unit, which in turn is part of a very large division. This concerns me because it appears to signal a loss in concern for those who serve in various capacities in churches and governing bodies. It has been said that this signals a shift in the denomination away from concern for church professionals, which was more evident in the seventies and eighties."

Surely the "resistance change creates" can be seen most clearly at the top of a hierarchical structure. It's harder to be a change agent in national church offices than at every other level (and I hear a similar dynamic experienced by my friends who work in government bureaucracies). While I empathize with the pain of those who are experiencing budget cuts at judicatory levels, I can't help wondering if it may not be more *useful* to have a higher percentage of financial resources invested at the local, congregational level.

Some Key Structures That Have Successfully Resisted Change

Mary V. Atkinson notes that "PCUSA reunion probably proves that there is resistance to change! Of course, the restructure which followed reunion made change necessary and irksome.

"The Presbyterian system makes change slowly. We have to go through committees and governing bodies at every level. While this has many good features, avoiding quick but erroneous decisions, it also makes us behind time on many occasions. Even in the local parish, the session has to have a called meeting if some decision has to be made. Decency and orderliness may mean the moment to act has come and gone before action can be taken. There may be a trade-off here: is it better to avoid poorly thought-out plans or to miss the moment? Of course, careful planning still can be shortsighted."

Fenhagen enumerates three key structures that have successfully resisted change in the following three sections:

The Affirmation of Ministry in the Marketplace

In earlier sections of the book the participants in our "case study group" and I have made some comments about the ministry of the laity in the world, and the difficulty of moving past verbiage to real change in the church power structures.

Members One of Another

Fenhagen outlines changes in canons designed to support greater "professionalism" among clergy and other reforms that failed because of an unwillingness to give up autonomy for the sake of the common good. Art Gafke responds:

"In the UMC the changes toward greater 'professionalism' of the clergy began to be shaped about the same time as for the Episcopal Church. In spite of the hopes that evaluative procedures would be helpful as a feedback loop, there was and still is great resistance to such feedback. Even now the wording of the Book of Discipline assigns, permits, and encourages various officers and groups of the church to evaluate the clergy. This has resulted in confusion and frustration.

"Of great hope in the UMC are those cooperative ministries, peer support groups, and caucus groups that give support and demand accountability. These groups vary considerably in style, setting, and purpose. In some conferences there have been conference-wide formation of peer groups with trained leaders. In many, perhaps most, of the conferences peer groups for probationary members of conference are mandated. These offer the possibility that the entering clergy will experience shared ministry in a supportive context as normative."

The Myth of Deployment

The "deployment" problems described by the author are shared by members of our case study group:

UCC: "The deployment/placement issues are almost carbon copies. We in the UCC are also frustrated with a system that takes twelve to eighteen months. The more conflicted situations we deal with, the more long-term intentional interims we need. Their work helps congregations feel less hurried in their search. From a clergy perspective, if one is in an untenable situation, anxious to make a move, the process is excruciatingly slow. Yet it is a mutual discernment process in which we truly trust that the Holy Spirit is at work. Often, congregations do choose just the right pastoral leader. Sometimes, they are not clear about their identity, needs, and expectations, or they do not do reference checks well, or they close their ears to the counsel of the judicatory, or they simply repeat the patterns of the past. And then we pull our hair out and gnash our teeth. But all we can do is pray that it turns out well anyway, or wait for the phone call from either pastor or people saying they've got trouble."

ELCA: "Again, many points of connection with our life in the ELCA. We do have a stronger system of deployment for our first call seminary graduates (I happen to be the person in the system with overall responsibility for the assignment process). My staff are giving more attention to assisting bishops and synod staff with clergy mobility; we are looking at development of more standardized call processes among the sixty-five synods and an electronic mobility system."

PCUSA: "The deployment, or call, picture varies for small churches over against large churches. It is quite difficult for smaller churches (particularly under, say, 150 members) to find or hold ministers. Yoking and tentmaking are options open to them, but aren't very popular, at least yet. Large churches tend to have many ministers interested in them, but the larger the church, the more choosey it can be, and this is often where age and gender biases appear most blatantly. Then, two-career couples and clergy couples also affect the call/deployment picture. Having to take two careers into account, whether or not both are in the church, has added new dynamics these last several years to the situations in which churches and clergy find themselves." These last comments by Mary V. Atkinson I hear from all the denominations I know.

Secrets, Pathology, and Gridlock

The members of our case study group have been learning from Edwin Friedman, too.

Triangles

The author puts it well: "With those who agree with me, I share the secret that I *know* who is out of step, although I have never spoken directly—or listened to—these 'out of step' others." Two of our responders identify triangulation as a problem in their systems. Says Michael Cooper-White, "Approaching the current situations from a systems perspective is refreshing. With the crisis management focus too many church leaders posit the problem as being (for example) 'the ineffective clergy.' This is the triangulation expressed as one of Friedman's principles."

Mary V. Atkinson notes: "PCUSA churches can certainly be said to show dysfunctional behavior in some cases. When triangulation takes place, the minister and church staff may get caught in the battle between factions or between individual members. Triangulation can be staff against staff, staff against member, faction against faction." And thus it goes in churches of any tradition.

Work with strength rather than weakness

Fenhagen draws a picture of bishops busy putting out fires and in the process appearing to value the "response to pathology over the reinforcement of strength." Wise parents learn not to reward acting-out children with lots of attention. Wise organizational consultants follow the same principle from family systems thinking. I remember a consultant who helped our organization through a sticky place some years ago. She could have focused on analyzing our problems. We might have derived some benefit through shovelling through all the mud in the hole we seemed to be stuck in. But instead this helpful consultant invited us to throw a rope out of the hole and climb out, by asking us, "What's your vision of the kind of organization you would like to have?" Instead of analyzing "who left *this* pile of mud here?" we came together in embracing a new vision for our future. I've never forgotten that meeting, and I take great pleasure in hearing our Alban consultants speak of applying that same principle in their work with congregations.

Art Gafke gives an interesting twist to re-visioning the executives' "burden of responding to misconduct"—a primary source of fire-fighting exercise for bishops and others. "Can we not also explore the dimensions of positive accountability forced on the church through the secular court system? That is, the church may be forced to do things in a manner that by Gospel mandate it should have been doing anyway."

Imagination Gridlock

Here the author returns to his hope, earlier expressed, that the church might speak to the culture, hopelessly trapped in "polarization between extremes." How do we ask new questions?

Art Gafke: "What are the economic and demographic pressures that afford the church an opportunity to frame new questions with new answers? In the UMC the small rural churches that were the strength of the denomination years ago are suffering with the massive movement from the farms to the cities and towns. With this population shift and the increasing costs of insurance programs for clergy, more and more part-time assignments are made to churches. Many of these are filled by a category called Local Pastors (lay persons with licensing and training who serve as pastors under the bishops' appointment.) The increase in the number of Local Pastors in the past seven years has doubled. In other areas of the country the influx of immigrant groups has resulted in many new churches and 'fellowships' being formed. Often the immigrant congregations are served by Local Pastors from their own communities. These pastors bring new opportunities as they offer problems which the formal, denominational structures cannot easily solve. Indeed new questions arise in these immigrant communities which can renew the church.

Having served most of my ministry in northern California, I am aware that natural and human disasters are normative. For any person a disaster is surprising and disruptive. For institutions disaster response can be more routine. Can we not form new questions regarding ministry in those places where there are and have been disasters? Do not the ministries of laity and clergy in the marketplace take particular power in these times? The church's sustained aid over a two-to-three-year period has been documented for its importance long after governmental and private relief agencies have terminated operations. Both clergy and laity in disasters forge new systems and patterns."

Mary V. Atkinson, too, was captivated by the idea of "imagination gridlock." "The Ordination Study asks for the PCUSA to use its imagination as it takes a new look at ordination. The question is, will the denomination be able to do this? Both prior denominations have a record of being unable to do much new with ordination. Several imaginative ideas have not fared well within the Presbyterian family: educator ordination, assessment in the new call system, clusters of churches sharing staff, to name three."

Structure Follows Mission as Form Follows Function

The Cornerstone project aimed at finding how "the structures of the church could more readily reinforce the gifts that clergy brought to the church's mission." Mary V. Atkinson had a different thought: "I've already mentioned the slow way in which change takes place in the Presbyterian system. Yet, sometimes we've seemed to want to solve our problems by redoing our structures. Less than seven years after a new denominational structure was inaugurated, it was dismantled and something new brought about. While finances were the driving force, the fact remains that the new structure wasn't even through with its shakedown cruise before it was sunk."

Finding Points of Connection

Fenhagen concluded from ELCA research learnings that providing help for pastors and congregations during their first year together could be a strategic move toward averting trouble later.

Davida Crabtree wrote: "I am keenly interested in the section about the ELCA work on mentoring with new pastors. Clearly times of transition are key opportunities for growth and change for both congregation and clergy. It is also the one point at which churches in the UCC are glad to have the help of the wider church. I have been thinking for some time about how great it would be if I could sit with each new clergyperson in their first week to talk together about their entry strategy."

Mary V. Atkinson adds: "The PCUSA has programs which bring together ministers right after ordination. There is no one model, but several, primarily now being carried out at the synod level. Some run for three summers, immediately after graduation/ordination. Others begin three years afterwards. Presbyteries also have mentoring programs, but I don't know how many or how successful."

Problems and Possibilities

In contrast to the Episcopal seminaries operating independently, and therefore feeling out of the loop and threatened, the PCUSA "denominational structure has had a way of bringing the presidents of the theological schools together, which means they hear from one another," reports Atkinson.

A Case for Systemic Change

Michael Cooper-White responds: "Your 'Case for Systemic Change' does not go far enough for me in raising the really radical questions. Beyond a shift from crisis intervention to prevention, is there a need to raise some very basic questions of stewardship. To cite one example: In the city of San Francisco, the ELCA has a dozen congregations with tens of millions of dollars tied up in real estate; the combined total weekly worship attendance in these congregations is fewer than 1,000 persons on an average Sunday. Is this good stewardship of the church's resources in an urban setting? Every congregation is 'budget poor and real estate rich'? What might happen if those parishes could capture a vision of corporate ministry that might include divesting of real estate in order to endow sustained community outreach? My impression is that most calls for systemic change point toward 'tinkering' rather than true transforming.

As a synod staff person, I spent thousands of hours over the years trying to help keep alive dying congregations. It was only in my last couple of years that I began to catch a vision that my call was to help them die gracefully and find new ways of engaging in ministry in a particular locale."

CHAPTER 6

The Spiritual Roots of Christian Leadership

With characteristic clarity, Max DePree defines what it means to be a responsible leader. "The first responsibility of a leader," he writes, "is to define reality. The last is to say thank you. In between the two, the leader must become a servant and a debtor. That sums up the progress of an artful leader."[1]

The distinguishing marks of all responsible leadership, therefore, is not only its quality, but its sense of rootedness. The ability to see things as they really are and to envision what they could be is not surface work, but the work of the Spirit within us. The mark of quality that distinguishes effective leadership from poor leadership comes from many sources and can be found in a great variety of people.

What distinguishes Christian leadership, however, is the sense of conviction about the source from which the gifts of leadership come and the purpose for which they are intended. The gifts of leadership that come from life in Christ are never given for self-aggrandizement or the manipulation of others, but to call forth the gifts that others have been given on behalf of the common good. Out of this essential rootedness the skills necessary for effective leadership must be learned.

The theological dimension of leadership is that which shapes our vision and our understanding of power. Without deeply planted spiritual roots, the energy that gives leadership its power to persuade others can all too easily become so dependent on external recognition that it loses touch with the self. Authenticity involves a connection between who we are and what we say. Authentic Christian leadership is leadership that draws its primary strength not from without but from within, where a sustained connection has been made with the Christ of whom we speak.

Without this our roots wither, and we lose that sense of authenticity that is life-giving to others and to ourselves as well.

Every ordained person I know struggles hard with the call to prayer, because deep down he or she knows it is important, even when difficult to sustain. Parish clergy find the call to prayer weakened over time by the seemingly endless demands of congregational life and their inability to set those boundaries that set them free. Nonparochial clergy often experience a loss of spiritual resolve simply because they lack a community in which the cultivation of the life in Christ is a meaningful priority.

There are, however, two identifiable blocks to a disciplined life of prayer that seem particularly evident in clergy. They can best be described as the loss of resolve associated with a sense of *entitlement* and unresolved feelings of *loneliness*. Effective response to these blocks, I suggest, involves embracing a spirituality of *relinquishment* and a spirituality of *solitude*.

Entitlement and a Spirituality of Relinquishment

The Bondage of Entitlement

Entitlement is a word used to describe the sense that we are owed something by virtue of who we are or the office we hold. *Entitlement* refers to our illusion that would have us believe we are entitled to all the good things that come our way and are entitled to use those who make these so-called good things happen.

One of the rewards of flying around the country, as I have done over the last two years, is the accumulation of an abundance of frequent flyer miles. I have accumulated so many bonus miles that I am regularly sent first-class upgrades. So when I am flying any distance, I am able to fly first class—a new experience in my life. But I have discovered that when I sit in first class on a plane, my attitude about the world can very quickly change. I feel a little superior to all the other people who walk past me to reach their seats in the coach section. It is a seductive feeling, reinforced by the way I am treated by the flight attendants whose job it is to help me feel this way. The cultivated feeling has something to do with that sense of entitlement that would have me believe that I deserve all this—that this is my due.

Feelings of entitlement block out gratitude and blind us to the depth of our own need. And the more public our lives, the stronger these feelings of entitlement can become if we are not aware of what is happening. As I reflect on my own life and listen to the stories of other clergy, I have come to believe that this sense of being entitled to special favors affects clergy to a far greater degree than is often acknowledged. Ordination seems to engender a sense that our public relationship to God and the things of the Spirit entitles us to some publicly endowed fruit, bestowed at minimal cost to ourselves. Clergy are famous for not replying to invitations or for saying that they will be present at a gathering and then not showing up. The feelings of entitlement that seem to accompany our living on center stage delude us into thinking that we don't have to live by other people's rules. We justify boundary violations, sensing that our own important needs justify our using others to meet them.

Entitlement is a spiritual issue of enormous consequence, for it deludes us into believing that because we talk about prayer, we don't really need to pray ourselves; because we lead others in worship, we don't need to worship for our own soul's sake.

But entitlement, like all illusions, loses its power when seen for what it is. Like all expressions of sin in human life, our claim to entitlement is but a disguised way of maintaining our need for control. Facing this squarely and honestly is a major step toward embracing the freedom the Gospel makes possible.

The Spirituality of Relinquishment

The biblical answer to the bondage imposed by entitlement is expressed most vividly in the relationship we see between Jesus and John the Baptist. Here is a description of entitlement turned upside down. When John the Baptist told his disciples that he must "decrease" so that Jesus might "increase" (John 3:30), he was freely giving up the need to control his own destiny so the power seen in him might be given to another. In a world where self-fulfillment and meeting one's own needs are highlighted as the keys to personal growth, self-relinquishment is not going to stir up much enthusiasm. The vocation offered to us in Jesus Christ, however, is precisely about losing our lives to find lives that are deeper and richer than we can produce on our own. I remember somewhere in

Sunday school being told that the Cross was an "I" with the "me" crossed out. It didn't seem like particularly helpful wisdom at the time, but given the values that shape our sense of identity today, maybe there was some truth there that we would do well to hear again.

Growth in Christ is directly proportionate to the diminishment of our need to maintain control over those aspects of life that affect us personally, particularly in situations where we perceive our sense of identity to be threatened. Relations between husbands and wives, between laity and clergy, between executives and their colleagues, between this group and that group, break down because we dare not risk anything that feels like loss of control. We are speaking, of course, of relinquishment that is freely given. Forced relinquishment is not relinquishment at all, but coercion. The free acceptance of relinquishment for the sake of others or as an expression of vocation is a mark of Grace. But this grace is blocked in our lives until we are comfortable with the freeing realization that we don't always have to be in control, that we don't always need to win, or that our self-esteem does not depend on being "center stage."

A spirituality of relinquishment calls us to find ways of leading that reinforce the giftedness of others. It is a life that points to Jesus Christ by affirming others and finding pleasure in their successes. A spirituality of relinquishment is a spirituality of trust that dares us to believe that the one who loses his or her life for Christ's sake will find it at a deeper level than has been experienced before.

Loneliness, Intimacy, and Solitude

Loneliness and Intimacy

In the last parish I served, my ministry involved preparing many couples for marriage, a ministry I both enjoyed and took very seriously. What I didn't enjoy were the receptions following weddings when the families of the couple were unknown to me. On such occasions I would put in an appearance, say "hello" to lots of people, and then leave feeling a bit depressed and possibly a bit guilty for feeling depressed. Since this feeling of loneliness occurred for me a lot while in the active parish ministry, I finally figured out what I think was going on. In preparing couples for marriage, I often experienced genuine intimacy as we talked through issues of profound consequence that touched my own life as well as theirs. At the reception, my role had drastically changed. The separation between us had already begun to take place, and we were establishing a new kind of relationship. The gap between the intimacy I had known and the realization that I was no longer needed in the same way was always an occasion of momentary loneliness—a longing for intimacy past.

Loneliness is a particular problem in the ordained ministry because we are forever moving between the experience of profound intimacy and the experience of intimacy lost. If not embraced as a necessary element in an effective ministry, these recurring experiences of loneliness can become a source of isolation and pain. Loneliness is the experience of absence, activated by the memory of what it was like being connected to someone who was important to us.

If our dominant memory of intimacy is one of mutuality where our sense of self is preserved, loneliness is easier to bear. If, however, our dominant memory of connectedness is one of dependence, seeking after the nurture we never quite got, loneliness is more intense because it is driven by the need to recover that which was never received.

When clergy speak honestly about stress in the ordained ministry, the subject of loneliness always seems to emerge. Yet *loneliness* is the secret word that is not much talked about in clergy circles.

Unless dealt with honestly, loneliness can be the force that drives us to seek release by substituting the illusion of intimacy for the real thing. This kind of substitute always comes out of dependency and reinforces it because it is instant gratification without the self-giving that is part of a genuine encounter. The sexual liaisons (both real and imagined) that too many clergy get invclved in almost always are born out of the need to relieve the pain of loneliness without cost to oneself. Like all other substitutes, these liaisons only serve to deepen the sense of separation within oneself (not to mention the hurt inflicted upon others).

The Gift of Solitude

Paul Tillich, in his now-classic sermon on the meaning of loneliness, points out that "our language wisely sensed two sides of the experience of being alone. It created the word *loneliness* to express the pain of being alone, and it has created the word *solitude* to express the glory of being alone."[2] Because these two experiences are so closely related, it is by embracing the experience of solitude that the pain of loneliness can become a source of healing rather than isolation and bitterness.

Sometimes at night, sitting in the living room with my wife after a long day, I have experienced a sudden flood of loneliness passing over me. Sometimes I share these feelings with my wife. More often I just take these feelings within myself until they seem to pass through and disappear. I have come to appreciate that experiences like this, as momentary as they are, provide the solitude I need to get in touch with myself after a day of extending myself for others. It is in embracing our aloneness that we are embraced by God. In that moment when we are most alone, the Spirit fills our center. In this space of solitude, our relationship with the risen Christ is reinforced at the deepest level of our being, freeing us to connect with others in ways by which we both are strengthened. Solitude is the seed bed of intimacy because it frees us to connect with others without needing to hold on desperately to ourselves.

Leadership and a Spirituality of Lament

Martin Marty, in a 1992 issue of *Context,* quotes a story told by Rabbi Lionel Blue; from a Jewish point of view it illustrates the living out of what I choose to call "a spirituality of lament."

> It was announced in Tel Aviv that God was soon to send a tidal wave thirty feet high over the city because of its sins. Muslims went to their mosques and prayed for a speedy transition to the paradise of Mohammed. Christians went to their churches and prayed for the intercession of the saints. Jews went to their synagogues and prayed, "Lord God, it's going to be very hard living under thirty feet of water."[3]

In many ways, our prayers for the intercession of the saints to the contrary, the call to exercise leadership in the Christian church today is a call to live with compassion "under thirty feet of water." A call to embrace a spirituality of lament places us squarely on the side of the victims of the world's pain. The cultural stimuli that bombard our senses would have us believe that happiness and a conflict-free existence is our right, something to be expected. When things go wrong or when tragedy strikes, we feel as if our normal life has been interrupted unjustly. A spirituality of lament is a spirituality of realism and connection; it recognizes that I can live a conflict-free existence only by cutting myself off from life itself; for most people in the world, pain and suffering are an everyday occurrence.

In his work on the Psalms, Walter Brueggemann has shown how necessary it is for the community of faith to own the grief, the dislocation, and the anger at God represented in the Psalms.

> The Psalter knows that life is dislocated. There need be no cover up. . . . It is the work of the one who prays a psalm to be actively engaged in holding this linkage in a conscious, concrete way. For when we do, we discover that this psalm is affected by our experience, and even more surprising, we find that our experience has been dealt with by the Psalms.[4]

A spirituality of lament grounds us in the real world, and only in the real world can one experience the hope of which the Gospel speaks. The pseudo-happiness our culture offers is a far cry from the hope the Resurrection proclaims. Our leadership in Christ is a ministry of hope, but it is a hope that emerges in confrontation with the world's pain. We were never promised a rose garden, but we were promised a relationship that sustains us through the turmoil and stress that is part and parcel of the challenge that life offers us. A spirituality grounded in this reality makes it possible for us to be both signs and bearers of hope to others.

Living as a Burden Bearer on Behalf of the World

Irenaeus, one of the early church fathers, described a priest as the burden bearer of the people of God. The ordained person, in his understanding, was one who willingly took on the burdens of others in order to call others to this ministry and to help people experience the limitless compassion of Christ. Saint Paul once wrote to the Galatians, "Bear one another's burdens, and so fulfil the law of Christ" (Gal. 6:2 RSV). The calling of the ordained person is to "so reflect" this law of Christ in his or her own life—so that ordination itself becomes a living invitation to others to share in the burden bearing of Jesus.

No one, no matter how saintly or how dedicated, is emotionally capable of bearing someone else's burden for long. For the Christian, burden bearing is never a solitary act. It is the way we participate in ministry of Jesus, turning over to him the weight of another's burden, so that the load we carry becomes more of an expression of love than of obligation. The world's burdens are made bearable when offered to the Lord. Jesus carries in himself what for us would be an impossible burden. If you have ever seen a picture of Matthew Grunewald's great altarpiece in the chapel at Isenheim, Germany (or seen the altarpiece itself), you can imagine something of what this means. Grunewald depicts Jesus on a cross with beams bending toward the ground, sagging with the incredible weight of the human burden that Jesus takes upon himself.

Christian leadership begins at the foot of the Cross. The meaning of vocation is tied up in our capacity to engage the world's pain, never alone but, always, as we pray "through Jesus Christ our Lord." "Come to me, all who labor and are heavy laden, and I will give you rest," Jesus says to us. "Take my yoke upon you, and learn from me; for I am gentle and lowly in heart, and you will find rest for your souls" (Matt. 11:28-29 RSV). When we are overcome by stress and can experience ministry only as obligation, this is the place to turn. For this is the invitation that takes us to the heart of ministry in Christ.

The call to be a burden bearer in the name of Jesus is the outgrowth of a spirituality of lament, and is expressed, I believe, primarily in three ways: as advocate, as intercessor, and as pastor. All three of these are interrelated, and all three are fundamental expressions of the rootedness that keeps leadership in the church both energized and visionary.

As Advocate: Compassion in the Public Realm

The ordained person and all others who share in the ministry of Jesus Christ represent Christ the burden bearer by bearing witness to the need for compassion in the public realm. Many people carry immense burdens that are more structural than personal: the homeless on the streets of our cities, the refugees from war and oppression who wander the globe seeking safety and shelter, and the millions of children who face a future without hope. The ordained person is called to hold before the church these kinds of burdens and the people who are broken by them, so that as a church we might bear some of the weight of this in our common life.

In recent memory has there been a time when the need has been any greater than now for men and women who will stand as advocates for the poor in the United States? The poor have become the enemy because they are a threat to the proportionately rich. The facts of welfare economics and the plight of the welfare recipients have been so distorted in the nation's political discourse that virtually no one is willing to speak truthfully or band together to search for desperately needed long-range solutions. To be a burden bearer means allowing ourselves to feel the pain of others; it means engaging the hopelessness of those the world would rather forget.

As Intercessor: Intercession as Mission

In the Episcopal tradition, the priest as intercessor and celebrant at the Eucharist serves as the burden bearer for the Christian community. Just as Jesus gathered all the world's brokenness and offered it on the cross to the Father, so are all our concerns gathered and offered with Jesus in the breaking of the bread in Eucharist. In every celebrated Eucharist, the intercessions of the people are gathered up and offered in unison with Jesus Christ's self-offering and transformed into a sign of his healing power. Nothing we do in the church is of any more importance. The eucharistic offerings that take place in every corner of the world are centers of energy that defy our imagination. As part of this intercessory community, Christians pray for one another and for the healing of the world. To pray faithfully for someone else or for some aspect of the world's pain, day after day and month after month, is a ministry of burden bearing that draws us to the heart of God.

Just before leaving New York City, where I lived for fourteen years, I had an unforgettable ride with a cab driver who unknowingly gave me a very special gift. During our drive into the city from La Guardia airport, the cab driver expressed his worry over his twenty-nine-year-old sister who had just found out she had a brain tumor. I was dressed in clerical attire, leading this man to believe that I was someone he could talk to. So he started talking nonstop in somewhat broken English, and I tried to listen, although fading in and out of the conversation as I wrestled with my own thoughts. When we stopped, the man turned to me, and said with a good deal of feeling, "Reverend, are you listening to me?" Energized by his confrontation, I said with equal feeling that I was. And he continued to talk, and I listened with all the energy I could summon. Finally he turned to me, hesitated, and then made this request: "Will you pray for her?" I said I would, and I did, with conviction.

But he did not know what he gave to me. By his request he helped me understand again who I am and what my life is about. He had asked me to bear his burden through my ministry of intercession, and in saying yes to him, God made me to him a symbol of hope.

As Pastor: Being Present to Others

Finally, the ordained person is a burden bearer by the way he or she reflects the presence of Christ in the personal interactions that go on in the life of a congregation. In his novel *Descent into Hell,* Charles Williams describes what he called "the practice of substituted love." In the novel a man actually takes on the burden of a friend. He feels the weight come upon him and he hears the cry of release as his friend is set free. Whether we can actually bear someone else's burden in such a concrete way as this, I don't know, but I do know what happens to me when someone is willing to listen deeply in those moments when the pain within me needs to be shared. I have always appreciated a thought offered by Henri Nouwen in *The Wounded Healer,* one of his first books on pastoral ministry. "Love not only lasts forever," he wrote, "it needs only a second to come about."[5]

In the role of pastor, the ordained person is asked to embrace the bearing of another's burden at its most personal level. And as most clergy discover very quickly, without a clear sense of one's own boundaries, burden bearing can be destructive to oneself and to those whose burdens we seek to carry. The aim of pastoral ministry is to help provide the immediate support that makes it possible for people in trouble to find within themselves through the Spirit the strength they need to cope with what faces them. Pastoral ministry is systemic in that it seeks to help build communities of healing in which the burden-bearing task in shared by many. Pastoral ministry involves the proclamation of the Gospel-Good News so that it can be heard and appropriated, for it is in embracing the Good News within ourselves that the heaviest burdens are made light.

The call to live as advocate, intercessor, and pastor in the community of faith is a way of life that finds its meaning in pointing always to the Christ who is our source of strength. In pointing to him, we are for others a living reminder. This is the meaning of Christian vocation, and when we lose touch with this meaning in our own lives, it is to the story of our redemption that we must first return. For as we are reminded, "The word is very near you; it is in your mouth and in your heart, so that you can do it" (Deut. 30:14 RSV).

A Spirituality of Gratitude

Not long ago I was told about a black South African priest who had come to this country to study in one of the seminaries of the Episcopal Church.[6] Ten years before, as a priest serving in an Anglican church in Soweto, he had been arrested by the South African police and imprisoned. For four years this Christian man endured unspeakable cruelty and hardship although accused of no crime. When he came to the United States some years later, he was asked by many how he had dealt with the rage he must have felt against those who sought to destroy his life. "I did feel rage," he said. "For some time I was overwhelmed by feelings of immense anger. But by the grace of God the anger has disappeared. Those four years have become for me one of the most important times of my life. During my imprisonment," he continued, "I received letters of encouragement from Christians all over the world, and especially from church people here in America. I am overflowing with gratitude, and, while I am here, I hope to contact all those people who wrote to me and tell them how grateful I am."

I am more and more convinced that the deepest and most enduring motive for prayer— indeed, the deepest and most enduring motive for embracing the ministry of Jesus Christ—is nothing less than sheer gratitude. I know without a doubt that in my own life the really important things have occurred solely through the grace of God: my children's well-being after much pain and struggle, my marriage of forty-five years, the gift of life itself made new every day. How do I make sense of this? How do I respond to that over which I have so little control? I don't know, except to embrace those deep feelings of gratitude that are within me that go beyond the words necessary to express them.

For some strange reason, honest feelings of thankfulness are often the hardest to express. I am aware as I visit different churches how quiet the responses are when prayers of thanksgiving are bidden during the intercessions of the people. It is as if we are embarrassed to say "thank you" to God, or maybe our resistance to our utter dependence on God's grace is stronger than we are willing to acknowledge. Faithfulness and longevity in ministry are the fruits of a spirituality of gratitude. For gratitude is a source of energy in itself, releasing in us love we didn't know we had.

Over the past two years I have spoken with many clergy about their struggle to establish disciplines of solitude and prayer that fit the reality of their lives. I have heard of the pain that comes when the faith we once professed in passion begins to lose its hold on us, of the guilt that is felt when preaching to others what we no longer feel ourselves. There are obviously many causes for the loss of faith, some internal and some external. Sometimes the way back into a living faith must begin with repentance and a new dimension of spiritual surrender. But most of the time, what is required is taking simple steps one day at a time.

The way back into a life of prayer is not by extra effort, but by participation in what God is already doing. Beginning to pray again is like putting one's foot into a moving stream and staying there long enough to feel the current and the energy it contains. "Spirit of God, pray through me," come the words. "Spirit of God, let me see." A simple prayer from the heart that connects us with the rhythm of the Spirit's prayer within us is all that is needed. "Spirit of God, breathe through me, Spirit of God, set me free; Spirit of God, let me live in thee." What in the beginning takes only a few minutes, phrases uttered spontaneously throughout the day, can reopen the doors to a deeper faith than we had before.

In a program aimed at helping to reinforce the life of prayer among the clergy of the Episcopal Church, the Cornerstone Project brought together groups of praying people who shared this concern to see what could be done to build stronger systems of support. It was interesting to note that when participants shared their spiritual journeys with one another, all acknowledged the importance of their connection with some formal spiritual center. For some, this connection was with a monastic community; others were tied to a more informal group concerned with the life of prayer that had stayed connected over many years. In subsequent gatherings the experience of being supported by others in situations of openness and trust became a common theme. The biblical affirmation that we are "members one of another" is not an addendum to faith, but a description of that way of life by which faith is deepened and sustained.

The Joy of Ministry

Much is being written about the difficulties encountered in the ordained ministry, with this book being no exception. But as many have testified, this is not the whole story. The many clergy who spoke of having found a deep sense of satisfaction in what they do and who they understand themselves to be represent a major segment of clergy in every denomination. Satisfaction in ministry is in some wonderful way related to finding joy in what we do. When we are stimulated by being with people who share with us a common vision, ministry can be just plain fun.

Yes, many evenings we go to bed tired from feeling overworked or disappointed, but on more evenings we go to bed with a deep sense of fulfillment for a day spent in doing what we love to do and doing it with a sense of creativity and competence. A faith that has been deepened by prayer that comes from a sense of need based on thankfulness; a genuine love of people; intellectual curiosity about ideas and problems to resolve; a yearning to see justice done in the world and deep feelings of compassion for those who have been hurt by the abuse of power; sharing with others that Gospel story that we have come to know; skills in working with people in ways that call forth their gifts; a sense of self that finds more pleasure in serving than winning—these are the ingredients of a ministry that ripens with the years. Some of these ingredients are learned, but most are gifts that come when we are open to receive them. Rigidity and control lead only to isolation and self-pity; creativity and flexibility are expressions of joy, and we find joy not as a reward, but in noticing and responding to the surprises of the Spirit along the way.

All Is Grace

In a beautiful and exceptionally wise article in *Weavings* titled "All Is Grace," Henri Nouwen writes:

> I am gradually learning that the call to gratitude asks us to say "everything is grace." When our gratitude for the past is only partial, our hope for a new future can never be full. As long as we remain resentful about things that we wish had not happened, about relationships we wish had turned out differently, about mistakes we wish we had not made, part of our heart remains isolated, unable to bear fruit in the new life ahead of us. . . . If we are to be truly ready for a new task in the service of God, truly joyful at the prospect of a new vocation, truly free to be sent into a new mission, our entire past, gathered into the seriousness of a converted heart, must become the source of energy that moves us toward the future.[7]

The ministry of the Christian church is indeed in transition. But where the roots are deep, hope abounds, and the challenges before us are seen not as threats but as signs of God's reign.

> The Spirit and the bride say, "Come."
> And let everyone who hears say, "Come."
> And let everyone who is thirsty come.
> Let anyone who wishes take the water of life as a gift. . . .
> Amen. Come, Lord Jesus (Rev. 22:17, 20).

The Spiritual Roots of Christian Leadership

Two members of our case study group talk about how clergy in their communions are struggling with those spiritual roots:

Art Gafke: "The current jargon of 'spiritual formation' represents a fairly recent acknowledgment in the UMC that we must reclaim the spiritual basis for ministry and life. Some of the jargon will be discovered simply as a new language system with which to continue business as usual. However, the encouraging reality in the UMC is the growing numbers of clergy and laity who are involved in spiritual disciplines as life (and organization) changing practices. Earlier I mentioned that the theme of the 1994 training of new superintendents emphasized their spiritual leadership. The resource materials for the Supervising Pastors and the Counseling Elders include the major framework of spiritual formation. The Supervising Pastor material which has been out for several years has been updated in the past few years to add this significant component. The Counseling Elder Manual is new this year and includes spiritual formation as the key ingredient in the mentoring relationship between the elder and the new pastor.

"The emphasis on discerning, celebrating, and responding to God's activity within and among us is a positive change in the cultural climate of our denomination. In some settings this bridges the chasms that otherwise exist between these polarities: control centered/Spirit centered, conservative/liberal, male/female, dominating culture/minority cultures, clergy/laity, rural/urban, older generation/younger generation. I am hopeful that the new spiritual culture growing in the denomination will include actions that carry long-term institutional change. Such change may indeed switch the normative culture to the inclusive, cooperative, mutual, and faith-based. Overwhelming the culture of isolation, competition, exclusivity, and fear is much needed."

Davida Crabtree: "I find no differences of substance in the value of this chapter for UCC clergy. We, too, urgently need to pay attention to our prayer, spirituality, and worship lives. We may be a little less likely to have a connection with a 'formal spiritual center' simply because there are few in our denominational heritage. Across the country, there is a cry for networks of clergy support. And there are early signs that clergy are beginning to take responsibility to support, nurture, and pray with one another rather than to believe that someone else should take that responsibility on for them." This fits with my recent experience working with UCC conference ministers gathered together. I was struck by the clear spiritual focus of their gathering and by the deep feeling in the group's worship under Bill Hulteen's leadership as well as the response to the guided meditation he led.

Entitlement and a Spirituality of Relinquishment

Our case study group members reflect on their own experience of clergy who seem to have a sense of entitlement:

Crabtree: "I am helped by your section on Entitlement and a Spirituality of Relinquishment. Often it seems that the clergy who feel most inadequate and powerless are the very ones who live out a scenario of entitlement. Feeling inadequate of course yields the need to control and to feel important. As soon as that happens, relationships become warped and ministries are damaged. (Gee, I thought it was only UCC clergy who didn't respond to invitations or show up when expected!)"

Atkinson: "We say that a theological degree and even ordination do not automatically guarantee a call to a pastoral or other position, but not everyone can hear that. It is always being said about that other person. I've certainly known ministers who feel their ordination entitles them to some special consideration. However I think that attitude is not quite as evident today. I have no facts to back that up, but it's a feeling I have. [I resonate with Mary's observation, and believe it's because clergy are much more uncertain of their role and of the esteem in which they are held by their congregations and the wider society. Authority is no longer automatically granted to them by their world in the way it would have been in previous generations. Where I do remember the playing out of a feeling of entitlement is in watching ministers come late to meetings and leave early. The unspoken feeling generated is 'I'm too important and too busy to stay around for this.'"

Gafke: "The material presented in this chapter fits well my experience of particularly the white male clergy population of the United Methodist Church. I believe that pastors of color and women would write the chapter differently. Those who come with a culturally built-in entitlement need to focus intensely on the spiritual costs of entitlement. Those who by reason of gender or race or language do not have entitlement may indeed experience life in Christ as itself an entitlement."

Loneliness and Intimacy

Mary V. Atkinson brings a somewhat more challenging approach to the ordained leader's experience of loneliness: "Ministers can be very lonely people. I wonder if this loneliness may be self-imposed out of insecurity? 'I am the holy person, therefore I can't let anyone know I am not totally secure and in control.' Do ministers really have to keep themselves at arms' length from both laypersons and from other clergy, or do they think they must? In my experience, men and women evaluate the clergy experience of loneliness differently. As I see it, men naturally tend to approach relationships with a bias toward separation as a value, while women more often assume a comfortable togetherness as the norm. We all have to live in the tension between self-differentiation and being-in-relationship, but men and women seem to assume different leanings in that tension. I see a lot of clergywomen, for example, moving pretty comfortably in and out of their role as it seems appropriate in different situations, while clergymen tend to take for granted (and sometimes even exalt) the loneliness of the role."

Being Present to Others

Mary V. Atkinson reflects on clergy and pastoral role of burden-bearing: "Many ministers move to pastoral counseling from the parish. I wonder if they find it easier there to have a sense of bringing healing. Can it also represent a desire to escape some of the more burdensome, tedious elements of parish work?"

A Spirituality of Gratitude

Davida Crabtree reflects: "Early in your book, you quoted one bishop as asking, 'How can we turn around the bitching, the denial, blaming the diocese and themselves?' At its foundation, this is a spiritual issue, and your spirituality of gratitude and grace addresses it directly. Now, of course, it has systemic elements as well, and so we might want to ask what an ecclesiological system built on a theology of gratitude and grace would look like. When we see the cup as half full instead of half empty, life, church, and ministry look different. What we experienced as threat we now see as challenge and opportunity. Fear transmogrifies into trust, and despair into hope. It isn't magic. It is entirely dependent on our spiritual rootedness, to use your terms. So when we are led by challenge, trust, and hope, our leadership in the Body of Christ is dramatically different than when we are led by threat, fear, and despair."

From the standpoint of a parish priest, Hollis Williams, a participant in the Cornerstone Project, provides a good example of "turning around the bitching" in a recent issue of the Alban journal: "Take responsibility for your ministry. Attitude is almost everything. There is too much complaining and blaming in institutions, especially in the church. Wake up every morning with this perspective: God is good, the church is good, people are good, the bishop or judicatory head is good. Massaging the flaws distorts us from the primary task of being faithful in the present moment and pointing to the kingdom that is always coming." (CONGREGATIONS, March-April, 1995, p. 19.)

All is Grace

Michael Cooper-White responds: "I appreciate Jim's ending on the note of grace (always music to the ears of a Lutheran!) I applaud his pointing us beyond the 'poor us' syndrome which may be too prevalent in our counsel to clergy and even our recruitment of candidates. This syndrome says in effect: 'Yes, ministry in the late twentieth century is hard. Bear your burdens. Pray and be grateful. Hang in there, partner!' Jim's ending 'gracenote' sounds another tone: 'No, doggone it, ministry is not just a burden. Ministry is downright fun—at least some of the time! It's a privilege given by God to a relatively few.' Imagine the privilege of standing before a group of folk and unleashing Jesus from the bread and wine into the guts and lives of people!"

A Case Study Method

A case study is the write-up of what James D. Glasse, in *Putting It Together in the Parish* (Abingdon Press, 1972), calls a "professional event," also called a "critical incident." By definition, a critical incident is an occasion in which the professional or leader acts as the responsible agent.

As a participant in a learning event, a professional or leader can learn from a critical incident by structured reflection on the event. The following is a structure designed to facilitate that reflection.

This structure has proven effective in a variety of learning sessions. It is a discipline that must be followed rigorously if it is to be useful. The case must be written and brief—**on a single sheet of white paper.** The limitation of space forces the writer to identify critical information. There are five sections to the case study. It is most helpful when the case study is organized in five paragraphs labeled with the headings used below.

1. **Background.** In this section provide enough information to put the case in context, including what you had in mind and what pressures and persons precipitated the event.

2. **Description.** State here what happened and what you, the reporter, did. Include as much relevant details as possible in the limited space, leaving out extraneous factors. Include those things that a group might need to discuss the case intelligently.

3. **Analysis.** In this section report what you, the writer, think is happening. Identify issues and relationships, with special attention to changes that took place. Indicate any turning points and when the event ended.

4. **Evaluation.** Estimate your own effectiveness in the event. Did you accomplish what you set out to do? Did you function effectively? Why or why not? Are there things you might have done differently? Where were the surprises for you? Identify issues you would like to hear the group discuss.

5. **Theological reflection.** Here briefly indicate how you, the leader, writer/reporter of the event, perceive God at work in the event. What does this event teach about human beings before God? How were you employing your theology as you were involved in the event? What biblical images come to mind?

Instructions to Case-Study Groups

Roles to Appoint (in each round of presentation)

Timekeeper/convener	Keeps the group on time and sees that it moves through the different phases of the process.
Presenter	Has enough copies of the case study for each group member.

Case-Study Process

Five minutes	Everyone reads the case. Make notes of things that are not clear or things to discuss.
Two minutes	Group asks questions of clarification. Presenter responds.
Fifteen minutes	Group analyzes, discusses the case. Presenter remains silent, taking notes if she or he wishes. Members probe for dynamics, hypothesize about what is happening in the situation. What kind of authority is being exercised here?

Suggest alternative ways of approaching the situation.

Two minutes   Presenter responds

Five minutes   Closing discussion of the case with opportunity for highlighting learnings, particularly by the presenter.

After two case presentations, take a break of fifteen minutes.

Chapter 1

1. Bernie Ghiselin, "Lashed to the Mizzen: Leadership in an Era of Turbulence," *Issues and Observations* 14, no. 2 (1994). Available from Center for Creative Leadership, P.O. Box 26300, Greensboro, NC 27438-6300.

2. Stephen L. Carter, *The Culture of Disbelief* (New York: HarperCollins, Basic Books, 1993), 3.

3. Robert Wuthnow, *Christianity in the Twenty-First Century: Reflections and Challenges Ahead* (New York: Oxford University Press, 1993), 120-21.

4. Carter, *The Culture of Disbelief*, 264-65.

5. William Raspberry, "Religious Right Acts as a Tribe," *Myrtle Beach Sun Times*, syndicated by *Washington Post*, November 8, 1994.

6. Diogenes Allen, "Spiritual Awakenings" (Paper delivered at the Consortium of Endowed Episcopal Parishes, Cincinnati, February 11, 1994), 4-5.

7. Loren B. Mead, *The Once and Future Church* (Bethesda, MD: The Alban Institute, 1991), 31.

8. Wuthnow, *Christianity in the Twenty-First Century*, 50.

9. Robert Wuthnow, *Sharing the Journey: Support Groups and America's New Quest for Community* (New York: Macmillan, The Free Press, 1994), 4.

10. Ibid., 18.

11. Ibid., 27.

12. Eugene H. Peterson, *The Contemplative Pastor* (Grand Rapids: Eerdmans, 1989), 77.

13. Max DePree, *Leadership Is an Art* (New York: Dell, 1989), 22.

Chapter 2

1. *Excellence in Ministry: The Personal and Professional Needs of the Clergy of the Episcopal Church*, Episcopal Church Foundation and The Alban Institute, 1988-89, 16.
2. Ibid., 14.
3. Ibid., 15.
4. Adair Lummis and Roberta Walmsley, *Healthy Clergy, Wounded Healers: Their Families and Their Ministries.* Available from Episcopal Family Network, 815 Second Ave., Room 400, New York, NY 10017.
5. James L. Lowery, "Report on the Research Effort on Well, Effective, and Thriving Clergy for the Cornerstone Project, Episcopal Church Foundation, 1991-92," 3. Available from Episcopal Church Foundation, 815 Second Ave., Room 400, New York, NY 10017.
6. Ibid., 8-9.
7. Ibid., 10.
8. Frederick Buechner, *Wishful Thinking* (San Francisco: Harper & Row, 1973), 95.
9. Speed Leas to Jim Fenhagen on The Alban Institute Involuntary Termination Research, January 5, 1993.
10. *Synagogy: A Progress Report,* May, 1993. Available from Cornerstone Project, 815 Second Ave., New York, NY 10017 or APSO, P.O. Box 18097, Knoxville, TN 37928.

Chapter 3

1. "Preface to the Ordination Rites," *The Book of Common Prayer* (New York: Oxford University Press, 1990), 510.
2. Ibid., 543; italics mine.
3. The theological statements prepared for the consultation were written by George Lindbeck of Yale Divinity School, Richard Norris of Union Theological Seminary in New York, and the Church of England theologian Stephen Sykes. Participants also read Joseph C. Hough, Jr., and John B. Cobb, Jr., "Professional Church Leadership" in *Christian Identity and Theological Education* (Chico, CA: Scholars Press, 1985).

4. H. Barry Evans, Grubb Institute, and Frederic B. Burnham, Trinity Institute, "Report of the Theology of Priesthood Project," prepared for the board of Cornerstone Project (August 3, 1993).

5. Stephen W. Sykes, "The Theology of Priesthood" (Paper distributed at The Theology of Priesthood Conference, 1991).

6. J. Robert Wright, "The Anglican Doctrine of Priesthood," *The Anglican* 24, no. 1 (1994).

7. Ibid., 1.

8. Ibid.

9. Ibid., 2.

10. Ibid., 3.

11. Henri J. M. Nouwen, *The Living Reminder* (New York: Seabury Press, 1977), 13.

12. Timothy F. Sedgewick, *The Making of Ministry* (Cambridge, MA: Cowley, 1993), 59-60.

13. Elie Wiesel, *The Gates of the Forest* (New York: Rinehart and Winston, 1966).

Chapter 4

1. Barry Evans, "The Idea of the Diocese and the Role of the Bishop as a Source of Life for the Parish." Available from Grubb Institute, 1047 Conestoga Ave., Bryn Mawr, PA 19010-1555.

2. Loren Mead, *Transforming Congregations for the Future* (Bethesda, MD: The Alban Institute, 1994), 84.

3. "The Ordination of a Bishop; The Examination," *The Book of Common Prayer* (New York: Oxford University Press, 1990), 517.

4. *The Ministry of Bishops* (New York: Trinity Institute, Trinity Parish, 1991), 8.

5. Ibid., 7-8.

6. Ibid., 19-20.

7. Leonora Stephens, M.D., *The Diocese of Dallas as a Family System,* 1994. Available from Episcopal Church Foundation, Room 400, 815 Second Ave., New York, NY 10017.

8. "The Ordination of a Bishop," *The Book of Common Prayer,* 517, italics mine.

9. Max DePree, *Leadership Is an Art* (New York: Dell, 1989), 145.

Chapter 5

1. Edwin H. Friedman, *Generation to Generation* (New York: Guilford Press, 1985), 23.

2. Edwin H. Friedman, "The Challenge of Change and the Spirit of Adventure" (An expanded version of two papers delivered during the week of October 12, 1992, on the occasion of the 500th anniversary of the discovery of America by Christopher Columbus), 6.

3. Davida Foy Crabtree, *The Empowering Church* (Bethesda, MD: The Alban Institute, 1989), 58ff.

4. *Deployment: The First 20 Years and Challenges for the Future* (A report of the Deployment Review Committee to the Board for Church Deployment, November 12, 1990), 8.

5. Margaret Wheatley, "New Science and the Learning Organization," *The Systems Thinker* 4, no. 10 (December 1993-January 1994). Available from Pegasus Communications, Inc., P.O. Box 120, Kendall Square, Cambridge, MA 02142.

6. Friedman, "The Challenge of Change," 9.

7. Ibid., 4.

8. Kent D. Fairfield, ed., *Recruiting for Leadership in Ministry: Challenges and Hopes* (A report to the Episcopal Church by a committee of the Board for Theological Education, December 1, 1993). Available from the Episcopal Church Center, 815 Second Ave., New York, NY 10017.

9. I note in particular the Charting the Future program established by the Church Divinity School of the Pacific, which involves "stakeholders" in planning for the future; the newly established Seabury Institute of the Seabury Western Theological Seminary, which focuses on work of congregations; and the Institute for the Practice of Ministry at the Berkeley Divinity School at Yale, which involves joint planning with congregations.

Chapter 6

1. Max DePree, *Leadership Is an Art* (New York: Dell, 1989), 11.

2. Paul Tillich, *The Eternal Now* (New York: Scribner's, 1963), 17-18.

3. Martin Marty, *Context* (July 15, 1992), 4.

4. Walter Brueggemann, *Praying the Psalms* (Winona, MN: St. Mary's Press, 1986), 21-22.

5. Henri J. M. Nouwen, *The Wounded Healer* (Garden City, NY: Doubleday, 1972), 67.

6. Rev. Jeffrey Moselane, who studied at the Episcopal Divinity School during the academic year 1992-93.

7. Henri J. M. Nouwen, "All Is Grace," *Weavings* 7, no. 6 (November-December 1992), 40-41.

Your Dialogue with

Ministry for A New Time: Case Study for Change

Study Guide by Jean M. Haldane

Published by The Alban Institute, Inc.
in cooperation with
The Cornerstone Project
A Ministry of the Episcopal Church Foundation

CONTENTS

Introduction   141

    How the Dialogues Are Organized   142

    Interviews in the Congregation   143

The Dialogues   145

    Chapter 1. Leadership in an Era of Turbulence   147

    Chapter 2. A Profile of Episcopal Clergy   150

    Chapter 3. Rethinking Our Theologies of Ordination   154

    Chapter 4. The Bishop and Diocese in a Time of Change: 157
                Reconnecting Function and Symbol
                in the Episcopal Church

    Chapter 5. The Case for Systemic Change   160

    Chapter 6. The Spiritual Roots of Christian Leadership   163

Interviews in the Congregation—Linked to Dialogues   166

Laity Groups Explore Ministry for a New Time   172

    Guide for Lay Groups   173

    Candidate Screening Committees,   174
    Committees on Ministry

    Church Boards, Vestries   175

INTRODUCTION

This study guide provides an interface between the experience of the reader and issues raised by James Fenhagen in *Ministry for a New Time: Case Study for Change.* When we review Fenhagen's text in the light of our personal vocational experience, new insights emerge. Not only that, we find ourselves evaluating these personal vignettes, even reassigning meaning to them. A reintegration of our total experience can take place.

Fenhagen has wisdom to share. From many denominations the comments of their representatives indicate that James Fenhagen's *Ministry for a New Time: Case Study for Change* has hit on core conditions of clergy life and work today. He writes from his own experience as ordained clergyman, as seminary dean, and as one who has listened intently to many, many clergypersons in a wide variety of settings. The value of his wisdom to clergy readers of all denominations can be greatly enhanced by this dialogue between your experience and your reading of this book. From this dialogue you will gain not only greater clarity and depth, but also ways to build coping strategies in an "era of turbulence" (Chapter 1).

The dialogue parallels the text, chapter by chapter. It suggests key vocational experiences to think about, perhaps share, questions for surfacing insights, and an interview format to use with laity. It addresses both the individual reader, as well as groups of clergy who can use the book for mutual learning and insight.

For Fenhagen it's crucial that the ordained are *set within the congregation.* So here we include a way for groups of laity to bring *their* experiences of call and ministry to the dialogue. Included also are outlines for use with screening committees, commissions on ministry, church boards/vestries.

When the suggested exploration is carried out with a group of ministers (clericus) the scope of the inquiry broadens. The speaker is listened to by colleagues who cannot only identify and empathize, but can also invigorate the discussion and help identify implications and strategies. The complexities of ordained leadership are tough enough, and some sharing of common insights can reveal paths that simplify. If a group of four or five clergy convenant to do this exploration, it would be helpful to have a convenor. The convenor can simply be the person you call if you can't make it! Or it could also be the one who looks over the next chapter's dialogue and guestimates what and how much the group might do. I envision the group exploration as basically self-directed but facilitation of some exercises might be helpful.

How the Dialogues Are Organized

While all Dialogues can be worked through on one's own, they generally are presented as ways to exchange ideas with members of a clergy group. Each Dialogue is planned for 1 1/2 hours of concentrated work (longer would be better). First the KEY IDEA of the chapter is highlighted. Then follows a format in which clergy can dip into their experience as is appropriate to the text. I introduce this with minimal explanation. This includes specific vocational experiences that you may bring to the text. *"Think of an experience when..."* Attention to the precise wording will yield a common base for understanding (in the group) of what is sought.

Individual readers can think of an experience and write about it and reflect on the questions.

NOTE: While the six Dialogues can be seen as one learning process, each Dialogue stands alone with its chapter.

LET IT BE ACKNOWLEDGED—the issues in Fenhagen's Case Study and highlighted in the Dialogue are *meaty*. Any one of them could usefully take a good deal of time. So more is here than can be accomplished, and you will have to make careful choices.

Interviews in the Congregation

Another layer in the learning process is a chance to connect with your daily ministry environment through 15 to 20-minute interviews with lay persons. The purpose of these is to check your perceptions about laity's experience and outlook in the church today. You will find an interview format linked to each chapter and to your Dialogue process in which you ask individual lay persons to share one experience which corresponds with or complements your shared experiences in the group. Individual readers may also interview the laity.

All this is to say that this learning tool is designed to help clergy and others get the most out of Jim Fenhagen's book—to identify their own learnings and determine any future action they deem appropriate.

The Dialogues

CHAPTER 1

Leadership
in an Era of Turbulence

KEY IDEA:
How are we doing in a time of great change?

Clergy respond in a variety of ways to what Fenhagen calls an era of turbulence. All the churches agree that ordained leadership is under great stress. How are you experiencing this? What are your dominant reactions, all the way from stimulating and energizing to downright discouragement and fear (what Fenhagen calls acedia)? Maybe you feel more than one of them—depending on the situation! The following suggestions for bringing your experience to bear on the text are linked to some issues, ideas, and concepts in this chapter.

Focus #1 What is your state of mind and heart? (50 minutes total)

• *Identify and describe one experience in your congregation (or other constituency) within the past year when you felt a sense of stability in an uncertain situation or a clarity of purpose amid much confusion of activity.* Each person takes 3 to 4 minutes. After each has shared, ask yourselves: *What kept you steady in an unsteady situation?*

• Do you see signs of discouragement in yourself as you go about leading the congregation? *Can you think of a particular experience that triggered a sense of discouragement—even despair—in you?* One of you share; others join in as it triggers their experience.
How are you coping with some heaviness of the spirit in yourself?

- How are the laity doing in these times of change?

  What evidence of stress-related reactions/behavior do you perceive in them?

  How are you currently responding to these signs of stress?

Focus #2 What contributes to turbulence? (30 minutes total)

Fenhagen names three "contributors." Choose one and use the questions to speak out of your own experience.

1) A lack of clarity around the church's mission

- Do you think the following statement is true? "The quest for a new moral center is the social agenda that lies at the heart of the church's mission—in the present and in the years to come." How does this statement compare with the general understanding of the church's mission in your congregation, judicatory, or national church? Write a paragraph in response and/or discuss with your colleagues.

2) The "New Laity"—a mixed blessing

- What blessings have you received in the "new laity"?
- What things cause you concern?
- Write and/or discuss. Try to give concrete examples.

3) The debate over scriptural authority

- Do you have Bible study groups in your congregation? Are there both "textual interpretation" people and "thematic interpretation" people? If so, does it cause problems? And how do you exercise leadership within what Fenhagen calls "The intensity of debate over what is biblical truth"?

  As you discuss, try to give short, pithy examples.

Final Discussion (10 minutes)

"What is one thing you need to do to ride out the turbulence and arrive at the other side of complexity—namely, simplicity?"

Quiet time, prayer, and/or what words, images in scripture that come to mind within context of your discussion? (Now look at "Interviews in the Congregation," p.15.)

Read Chapter 2 for next time.

CHAPTER 2

A Profile of Episcopal Clergy

KEY IDEA:
What does it take to thrive as an ordained leader in these times of change?

Here Fenhagen tells of deep satisfactions and well-being experienced by many clergy, and at the same time vulnerability and role confusion experienced by others. There are "thrivers," those who are "OK" but at risk, those who are "in trouble."

Focus #1 What are the satisfactions in the ordained role?
(45 minutes)

• *Think of several experiences in your ministry in the last five years that you would call satisfying—experiences that felt congruent with your sense of call. Jot down a few notes about these experiences. Select one —the most satisfying—and describe it to the other members of your ministerial group. Each take three to four minutes to share.*

After telling and listening, ask yourselves "What made these experiences satisfying for us as ordained leaders?" Discuss. "Given these descriptions of what is satisfying for us, how close are we to traditional understandings of the ordained role, and at what points do we expand into fresh perceptions of ministry? And what understandings of our role do the laity seem to have? What kind of hopes, hungers, and yearnings of the spirit get expressed in relationship to us—their pastor?"

Focus #2 What are your particular strengths for ordained leadership? (25 minutes)

• *Think of an experience in the last year or so when "you felt you did something well, enjoyed doing it, and were proud of it."* It could be anywhere in your life—work, family, community, in or outside the church.* Individuals write a brief description. The small group breaks down into pairs and trios. Each person shares 3 to 4 minutes.

Reporting on your research (10 minutes). Best done at the beginning of the Dialogue session.
• Review and discuss the two interviews about the degree of "acedia" in your two lay persons. Did you get new insight? Did the interviews encourage or discourage you?

Then the other persons in pairs and trios can suggest a strength they hear demonstrated in the experience. This is simply a way of reminding one another that everyone has strengths. Some may want to explore this further at another time.

Everyone rejoins the group and responds to "How are you using your strengths in your present ministry?"

Focus #3 What factors contribute to your well-being now?

It may be possible to do the checklist in the remaining time. The questions can be mulled over at home and may be discussed with another colleague or friend.

*Copyright Bernard Haldane, *Career Satisfaction and Success*

CHECKLIST: Contributors to Health

Estimate how you are doing on the following scale taken from the Clergy
Family Project Study, page 36 of *Ministry for a New Time*. Circle one on
each scale.

I am doing well in terms of:

		Weak				Strong
1.	Consistent quality time with spouse or close friend	1	2	3	4	5
2.	The absence of major problems or the ability to deal with them	1	2	3	4	5
3.	Being able to successfully establish clear boundaries between congregational duties and private life as well as appropriate boundaries in interpersonal relationships	1	2	3	4	5
4.	Satisfactory private and social life	1	2	3	4	5
5.	Professional self-concept	1	2	3	4	5
6.	Being able to live comfortably on my income	1	2	3	4	5
7.	Regular exercise	1	2	3	4	5
8.	A good prayer life	1	2	3	4	5

After you have completed the scale, make a few notes around some of
these questions:

In general, how do you feel about the profile you see? Look at the
strong(er) items as a group—what does that tell you? Look at the
weak(er) items, where does the emphasis fall? Is there a surprise for

you? Are these long-term habitual ways of living/working? Or have some new factors "snuck up" on you?

In view of your role as ordained leader and the current situation in your congregation or other place of ministry: Are you doing well? As well as is possible? Not too well? Limping along? Is there one thing that needs attention NOW? What steps could you take to strengthen your leadership?

• *Finally, this important discussion needs to take place—at another time.*

What is needed in the church system (as a whole) to provide encouragement for those who are doing well, support for those who are OK but "at risk," and help to clergy in trouble?

Quiet time, prayer, and/or what words, images in scripture come to mind within context of your discussion? (Now look at "Interviews in the Congregation," p. 16.)

Read Chapter 3 before the next meeting.

CHAPTER 3

Rethinking Our Theologies
of Ordination

KEY IDEA:
What contributes to our understanding and image of ordained
ministry?

Fenhagen says that there are relatively clear understandings of what ordination means within the various denominations. Moreover these theologies have changed very little over the years. In contrast, "The actual
practice of ministry has changed radically." So there is a discrepancy
between theory and practice.

Focus #1 "So why is my role confusing?" (45 minutes)

• Fenhagen lists three factors that contribute to role confusion:
1) theological time lag, 2) baptismal ministry, 3) loss of status in society.
Use #1 for description and discussion. Think about #2 and #3 outside the
group or make a note to address these at another time.

1) Theological time lag: Think of your ordination. Describe in
writing or verbally to one another. What did you feel was happening to
you and for you? What do you think was the message to the laity who
congregated for your ordination service? Take three or four minutes
each.

Then, do you see any attitudes or practices in your ministry that
stem in part from that experience? If you were ordained today, what
would you change and what would you retain in the Ordination Rite to
represent more clearly the role of a minister/priest and his/her relation-

ship to the whole church? What could be said or done to bring the theory of ordination and practice of ministry closer together?

2) *Ministry of all the baptized:* **Think of an experience when lay** *expectations of you were at odds with what you consider to be your calling, your role. Where do you think these expectations come from? How have laity come to have these expectations of you?*

3) *Loss of status in society:* **Think of and list the small and large** *ways in which the message gets through to you that being a minister/ priest is no longer accorded respect and honor— automatically—in our society. Is this just clergy or are other professionals having this experience? Is this a message about the nature of authority and leadership? Talk with attorneys, doctors in your congregation.*

Focus #2 Is what I do in ministry worth doing? (15 minutes)

•   Clarity about our calling can contribute to our sense of worthwhileness. *Write in twenty-five words or less your response to these questions:* What is the meaning of ordained ministry for you? What is your basic frame of reference? What do you draw on in biblical terms? Who do you look to for your understanding (theologian, seminary professor, other?) In twenty-five words or less what is the nub, the kernel of the ordained role for you? Take 5 or 6 minutes.

Read out loud to the other members of your group. Do not discuss at this time—in other words no "cross-talk," no response or feedback. Simply listen when it is another's turn. Go on with the rest of the Chapter 3 Dialogues, leaving your twenty-five words to be looked at later, and to be edited if necessary to make them descriptive of your experience, how the words are true for you.

Reporting on your research (10 minutes). Best done at the beginning of the Dialogue session.
•   Review interviews in the congregation. How did the laity look or seem as they were telling about what they do well and love to do? What implications might there be for ministry in the church and beyond?

If you are running short of time, I suggest that you go directly to Focus #4 and save #3 for another time, or for back home reflection.

Focus #3 How do you arrive at your definition of priesthood/minister?

Which historical layers, as Fenhagen sets them out, do you feel best express your theological understandings and your practice of ministry? Is there a layer missing or a historical turning point that is not a part of the six layers referred to in Chapter 3? Make a note on how and when you share your thoughts and convictions with your colleagues. Interdenominational groups of clergy will have a lot to share!

Focus #4 What do you expect of yourself as a priest? (20 minutes)

•   *Fenhagen speaks of Servant Leadership, Keeper of the Flame, Living Reminder. Do any of these words embody the passion and power you feel for your calling? Share with each other.*

Quiet time, prayer, and/or what words, images in scripture come to mind within context of your discussions? (Now look at "Interviews in the Congregation," p. 17.)

Read Chapter 4 before next meeting.

The Bishop and Diocese in a Time of Change: Reconnecting Function and Symbol in the Episcopal Church

KEY IDEA:
Who are bishops and how do they fit into the day-to-day life of the church?

The problem of declining influence of judicatory structures is not unique to the Episcopal Church. Oversight and authority are not easy role functions, especially when combined with a pastoral function. Is episcopacy a strength in the church today?

Focus #1 Who is the bishop for your congregation? (45 minutes)

Fenhagen points to the bishop's role being seen as functionally irrelevant, and symbolically without power these days. Before getting into a discussion, do the following exercise. It will bring out the key issues through your experience.

• *Think of the last time the bishop (conference minister, district superintendent, etc.) came to your congregation. What was the occasion? How did you prepare for his or her visit? How did you describe to the congregation what the bishop would do? Did you feel some necessity to explain what a bishop is? How did you say that? Do you have some hopes for what s/he would do beyond the agreed upon "agenda"? Who actually met the bishop? What was the impact of his/her visit upon the congregation? Did s/he do what you hoped for? Write a few notes on this visitation.*

One or two clergy share their experience. The others describe anything that was *different* in their experience of the bishop's visit.

Then, what can we say about the role of bishop, as it is now? What is our relationship with the bishop? Would you prefer s/he be primarily *your* pastor, there in times of conflict? What is laity's view of the bishop? Does it matter how they view the bishop?

Focus #2 Do you have a compelling vision of the worldwide church?

The bumper-sticker "Think globally. Act Locally" sounds good. Is it possible to do both? "Mission on our doorstep" (Loren Mead) is a challenge to local action. Is it possible to stay open to the large mission of the combined Christian churches and to derive strength, patience, and inspiration for our own local effort?

• *Think of an experience when you were part of some religious worship service that was far larger, more inclusive, more powerful than you normally experienced. Maybe it was when you went to a church camp or a youth conference, an interdenominational conference, an international gathering of your denomination, or something else. Describe the scene and how you felt. Each share three or four minutes. Then, what was the impact of this experience for you? How did it impact your sense of "church"? How did it impact your membership in the local congregation? Would you say you were thinking more globally as you were acting locally?*

Reporting on your research (10 minutes). Best done at the beginning of the Dialogue session.

• If you did a congregational interview, take five minutes at the beginning to review it. "What did laity say about authority of baptism for their lives? How does it compare with your sense of the authority of ordination?"

Focus #3 Symbol of bishop as source of empowerment for mission of the church. (25-30 minutes)

Fenhagen speaks of the need for connectedness between bishop and congregations. What would it take to develop "a deep enough level of intimacy and honesty for trust to emerge"? Should the bishop be teacher, pastor, partner with you and the congregation rather than largely being seen as regional administrator?

•   *Using the symbol of the bishop's chair—how could this largely out-dated symbol become one of connectedness? (Fenhagen suggests some ways.) How could it once again symbolize the presence of the bishop—the Servant Leader...How could this chair become a humble seat and not a throne? How could this chair become the seat of—not power—but empowerment?* Discuss what you could do toward reconnecting function and symbol in the bishop's role.

Quiet time, prayer, and/or what words, images in Scripture come to mind within context of your discussion?

Read Chapter 5 for next time.

CHAPTER 5

The Case for Systemic Change

KEY IDEA:
"In Christ all things hold together," yet "The church isn't working"...?

Fenhagen points out that the church is at one and the same time the body of Christ—all parts interdependent and interrelated—and a fallible human institution in which even desired change is resisted, often short-lived, and "change that does occur was unintended."

Focus #1 Homeostasis or change creates its own resistance
(40 minutes)

• Begin by dipping into your own experience of change. *Think of an experience in which you and others were working for some specific change in your congregation—and the resistances you experienced, whatever the final outcome. It may have been a change involving worship, music, some structural changes in the church building, scheduling—whatever. Each briefly tell of the specific change you were working on, the people "for" it, and how the resistance was expressed, how it affected what you were able to accomplish and final outcome. Take five minutes each.*
    When all the stories have been told, see if you can relate them to one or two of Fenhagen's categories. For example, was it a change where the stakes were high? Were there potential winners and losers? Or did you

communicate, communicate, COMMUNICATE about it until you felt
the change must be happening? Or did you or others resort to "lessen
anxiety by bonding with someone else in a way that makes a third person
the problem"?

Focus #2 Imagination Gridlock: Working from Strength
(25 minutes)

Fenhagen writes of our need to look at the whole church system and the
world around us with a wide-angle lens, and to approach new problems
from a standpoint of strength.
• *Discuss: What strengths are there—in my congregation, my
denomination, myself? What does our congregation do best? What
strengths can we build on?*
    Then, *how can we become sensitive to incremental change— how
can we read the signs of it, so that we adjust our course? Can we be
open to unintended change—ready to see it as opportunity?*

Focus #3 Great changes? Well, yes and no. (25 minutes)
You may have to postpone this...

Fenhagen writes about changes in the church that didn't happen or only
half-way happened in relation to both clergy and laity's ministry.
    Pick up on *one* of Fenhagen's examples, namely: *Affirmation of
Ministry in the Marketplace, Members One of Another, the Myth of Deployment.* Discuss. How does this play out in your congregation or
diocese-judicatory? What role do you have in it? Perhaps one member
of the group would start off and others join in as they are reminded of
their situation.

Reporting on your research (10 minutes). Best done at the beginning of the Dialogue session.
•   Review what you gleaned from the church membership his-
tories. Do you feel that when people have belonged to several
denominations, they may lack formation in any one tradition,
leading for some laity to a reasonable lack of interest in the
larger church or the bishop's role?

Quiet time, prayer, and/or what words, images in scripture come to mind
within context of your discussions? (Now look at "Interviews in the
Congregation," p.170.)

Read Chapter 6 for next time.

CHAPTER 6

The Spiritual Roots of Christian Leadership

KEY IDEA:
How do we maintain congruency between what we teach others and what we practice ourselves?

"Authentic Christian leadership is leadership which draws primary strength—not from without, but from within where a sustained connection has been made with the Christ of whom we speak." (Fenhagen)

Focus #1 Struggles in the spiritual life of a pastor/priest.
(40 minutes total)

Fenhagen speaks of very personal issues in the spiritual life of a minister/deacon. He points to Entitlement and Loneliness as being particularly crucial to recognize and to resolve with Relinquishment and Solitude respectively.

- **Entitlement—Relinquishment** (20 minutes):
  Think of an experience when you felt an assumption or expectation of a church member did not fit with your own sense of what your priesthood is about. You felt perhaps your vocation diminished, your role devalued. Each write a few notes on that experience. Then one or two describe their experience. Others respond, adding their own experience as appropriate.

  Then ask yourselves, "Was a sense of 'entitlement' part of our experience? What was reasonable in our reactions? What is it we feel entitled to because of ordination?" Try to be specific. Do you experience

this as a problem? What would it take to relinquish your sense of entitlement? To "decrease that Christ may increase"? Share, discuss.

Reporting on your research (15 minutes). Best done at the beginning of the Dialogue session.
- Review interviews of the laity in past week. How did you feel about their ministry and its risks "beyond the walls"? How do you react to the church's NO-CHANGE on laity's ministry in the marketplace. Then reflect on the five interviews with the laity. What did you get out of them? What insights, questions?

- **Loneliness—Solitude** (20 minutes):
Fenhagen shares his own experience of loneliness. What is your experience? *Each write a few notes on a specific experience when you had a deep sense of loneliness. It may be an experience that recurs, possibly triggered by similar circumstances; if so, choose one of those many experiences and try to describe it in detail, what preceded the feelings, how it felt, what you did about it—if anything.*

A different pair (or maybe just one person) describes their experience. Others, as before, respond out of their personal experience.

Then "Does loneliness go with the territory when you are a vocational 'religious'? What does it take for loneliness to be transformed into solitude?"

Focus #2 Burden-bearer on behalf of the world. (15 minutes)
(THIS FOCUS IS IMPORTANT but you may need to go to Focus #3 in order to finish the Dialogue satisfactorily.)

Fenhagen sees this function of ordained ministry, expressed as Advocate, Intercessor, Pastor.

Each choose one of these that you feel strongest in and write a short paragraph describing what you do as Advocate or Intercessor or Pastor. Assume a reader or hearer knows nothing about this aspect of your vocation.

Read off to the group (or by yourself), while the others listen, no cross-talk, no discussion. You may want to follow up with conversations about these areas of your strengths.

Focus #3 Ordained leadership in an era of turbulence. (20 minutes)

Use the following questions to bring these six sessions to a close.
1) What gives joy to you in your ministry? One word or phrase!
2) What have you to be thankful for? One word or phrase! 3) What moments of grace have these past weeks of reflection on *Ministry for a New Time* brought? Name those "moments." 4) What hopes do you have for weathering the turbulence, and helping your folks to do the same? What might you *do* to help those hopes become real? Share/ discuss.

Quiet time, prayer, and/or what words, images in scripture come to mind within context of your discussions? (Now look at "Interviews in the Congregation, p.171.)

Interviews in the Congregation– Linked to Dialogues

Purpose. To assist you to begin translating some of your explorations in *Ministry for a New Time* into work with the laity...in order to promote good relationships, ease tensions, build laity more able to cope with change in partnership with you.

The interviews are 15 to 20 minutes each, to be done *after each of your dialogue meetings/readings.* Basically, you ask laity to share one experience that corresponds in some way to the experiences you have identified and shared in your clergy group. Your job is to be precise about the experience you want, then listen, affirm their helpfulness, keep open the possibility of more interviews.

Discussing the interview questions in your clericus group can be of additional value to you, as will be short reviews of the interviews (in the Dialogues).

CHAPTER 1: Leadership in an Era of Turbulence

Interview Questions: How stressed are the laity?

The purpose of this interview, as related to Chapter 1, is to check your perceptions about how lay people see change in the church and in society (albeit a tiny sample).

As this is the first interview, it is important that it be positive and thought-provoking for the laity and for you. Also that the details be done well? So it is spelled out a little more than the rest of the interviews. Interview two lay people (separately), one in a leadership role in the congregation, the other not. Don't choose your main supporters or greatest critics, but perhaps folk you don't know so well.

Briefly tell the lay people what the purpose of the interview is... example: "A group of clergy, of which I'm one, are exploring the nature of the church and its mission today, and our role as clergy. We would like to get input from one or two of our laity. I wonder if I might 'interview' you about your experience in the church today...about 15 to 20 minutes." When you meet, repeat the purpose of your meeting and say you'd like to take a few notes. "And please know there are no right or wrong answers–just your experience."

Ask the individual *"Will you share with me just one experience in the church over the past year that was satisfying in some way, perhaps nurturing or strengthening?"* If the response is brief ask "What exactly happened for you?" If too general, ask "Could you give me an example?" Listen. Thank the person. The telling of this experience will put the lay person in touch with a basic value and meaning (stability) regarding his/ her membership in the church. This is the context for moving to less positive things.

Second questions, "What is one thing that worries/concerns you about the church today?" Try to get a brief example. Third, "What is one thing in society that especially bothers you right now?" Listen. Here you are checking for signs of discouragement in this lay person. After the response, thank him/her and say, "May I check with you again in the next few weeks if I need to?"

CHAPTER 2: A Profile of Episcopal Clergy

Interview Question: What strengths do laity have for "ministry in a new time"?

The purpose specific to chapter 2 is to get a glimpse of two to four people's strengths that shape their ministry. It is suggested that you ask the two persons, plus another two. Continue to have a balance of leaders and members. Interview them separately 15-20 minutes each. If the extra time is not feasible, stay with the same two people.

Repeat the purpose of the interview (see Chapter 1 Dialogue), also "no right or wrong answers." Give opportunity for brief comments about the first interview.

Ask, "*Think of an experience in the last year or so, when 'you felt you did something well, enjoyed doing it and are proud of it.'** *It could be anywhere in your life—work, family, community, in or outside the church.*" Repeat the three-fold definition, "*you felt you did something well—and it's your feeling that counts—enjoyed doing it, and are proud of it.*" Wait. Listen. Say "thank you."

Then, "You know, one strength I think you must have used is _____" (whatever you hear as an obvious one). "Of course there are more—all gifts from God." Then "How do you feel you are using your strengths, your gifts—in the church?" Listen. Say "Thank you."

If you wish, you could conclude your interviews with the original two persons at this point. If you are not sure simply say "I do appreciate your thoughts, time, etc. I hope I can call on you again if I need another interview? Thanks." Ask the second pair (if you have them) to be available for another interview.

Chapter 3: Re-Thinking Our Theologies of Ordination

Interview Question: Where do laity find authority for their calling?

The purpose specific to Chapter 3 is: To test the authority baptism has for lay people's sense of Christian vocation.

Now it is suggested that you ask four lay people (if you had four last time, drop two, add two new ones), again 15-20 minutes each. (Repeat overall goal for the two new ones.) Get into it this way: "Baptism has become more prominent, or central, in the Episcopal church and many other denominations. I want to focus on it now."

Do you remember your own baptism—or were you too young? Have you participated in a baptism? Lately? Think of one baptism where you were present. How would you describe it? Listen. Then, "*What words caught your attention? Perhaps words of the parents, godparents: perhaps the vows? prayers?*" Listen. *What actions of the clergy? How did you, or do you, feel about your role in the ritual*

---

*Copyright Bernard Haldane, Ph.D., *Career Satisfaction and Success* *as a member of the congregation? What feelings do you have about the rite of baptism? What part does it have in your sense of the church? How does it shape your own ministry? What authority does baptism have for your life?"*

Some of these questions will evoke comments, some not. Pause between questions to give time for thinking and responding. Thanks to them, ask new interviewees if you may call on them again.

CHAPTER 4: The Bishop and Diocese in a Time of Change: Reconnecting Function and Symbol in the Episcopal Church

Interview Question: What has led to a parochial view of church and bishop's role?

The purpose specific to Chapter 4 is: To explore the possibility that belonging to a number of denominations in their lives may mean their greater effort is put into a local congregation, with little or no appreciation for the church beyond. The same four (if time permits) or the latest two lay people should be asked for separate 15 to 20 minute interviews. Explain overall purpose again. If you have found note taking helpful, say again, "I'd like to take some notes."

When you meet, get into it this way, *"It seems that each denomination can point to many of their members coming from other denominations. So, many people have a varied 'church history.' Would you tell your church story—starting from the beginning? For example, "I was born into a Methodist family..." You can go through it quickly but try to remember the different churches you belonged to."* Listen.

Ask, "What was something you valued in some of these church experiences? Did you get involved or know much about the regional or national church? How did the bishop, moderator, conference minister appear to be significant to your congregation or to your priest, minister? What attracted you to the Episcopal (PCUSA, etc.) church?"

If you get a "cradle" Episcopalian (Methodist, etc.) focus on history within that church. Ask "What do you remember most about growing up in the Episcopal Church?" Then "How have you experienced the diocese?" "What role has the diocesan bishop played in your church history?"

Thanks for their faithfulness in a number of church experiences.

CHAPTER 5: The Case for Systemic Change

Interview Question: Whatever happened to ministry in the marketplace?

The purpose specific to Chapter 5 is: To pick up on one hoped-for change in the Episcopal Church and many others, namely the importance of laity's ministry in the marketplace, described by Fenhagen as never having been embraced and made operational by the church. This interview could give a glimpse of lay persons acting in light of their Christian vocation "in the world."

Choose two new lay persons—again individual interviews, 15-20 minutes each. Repeat your purpose of lay input to the clergy group. This might be a way to begin: "We often talk in the church about ministry in the world—meaning your daily life—in the family, your work, community, and so on." Ask: *"This question asks you to go beyond the walls of the church, to focus on your daily activities. Will you think of a time, an experience, when you felt compelled to speak or act— and did! —simply because you felt it was right?"*

The experience you are asking for is an unusual one for us to ask the laity. One, or both, may say they cannot think of anything. You can help them to let the experience surface by saying something like "This doesn't have to be anything global, though it might be!—perhaps an incident in your work, or with your kid's school, or on a committee, or in the supermarket." Then report, *"When you felt you should speak— say something—or act—do something—(and* did*) simply because you felt it was right."*

Listen. Then, "What was the risk for you in doing this?" Listen. Then, "What supported you in doing this?" Listen. "Thank you. Glad you are out there."

CHAPTER 6: Spiritual Roots of Discipleship

Purpose of interview related to Chapter 6: To help lay people to talk about their spiritual lives, how they are alive and what difficulties they may encounter. Same two people from last interview—15 to 20 minutes. Get into it something like this: *"The church teaches that to carry out our discipleship or ministry we need spiritual nourishment. Prayer, Bible-reading, meditation are some traditional ways to become centered on God. Think of an experience in which you felt centered on God, close to God. You might think of it as being a spiritual or religious experience. It might involve prayer or something else. It might be part of your daily life, perhaps not. Other people could have been involved, or perhaps you were alone. An experience in which you felt centered on God—momentarily or over time."* Listen. Then ask about small disciplines that people may have devised for themselves: "Is there something you always do, for example, some people always say grace before meals?" What difficulties are there in 'centering' God"? Listen. Thanks.

Laity Groups Explore Ministry for a New Time?

Obviously this is a book addressed to clergy, so how could it benefit laity to read it and how could it benefit clergy to have laity read it?

One benefit for clergy is that Jim Fenhagen says things that are difficult for them to say! For example he highlights not only the blessings of the "New Laity," but some of the problems. A benefit for laity is Fenhagen's insights vis a vis the historic and developmental role of the ordained, as well as his indicating the scale of change in the church with its attendant confusions in role and mission.

Change affects us all. Clergy and laity may each get their head and psyche and spirituality around these changes so they feel more comfortable, steady, and confident. But if they are not talking, conversing, having dialogue with some of the same books, and each other, old expectations and assumptions will remain and the ability to cope with change and move towards mutuality of ministry will be severely hampered. Jim Fenhagen's book sets the ordained role within the church congregation, not apart from it. So, while the primary focus of the book is the ordained role, the whole church is the setting, the raison d'être.

Invite one or multiple groups of four to six laity to read and reflect on *Ministry for a New Time*, using this Dialogue format as possible, the aim being to clarify the role of the ordained as it relates to the whole church. And why not have these going while you are in your clergy group doing it? (Though it may get a bit hectic along with the interviews? It will need weighing.)

Guide for Lay Groups

A convenor for each small group would be helpful (as described for clergy groups).

The convenor along with the priest or pastor can develop a list of laity who are invited to participate in the six dialogue sessions of 1 1/2 hours. It will be helpful if the convenor(s) plan how to use the clergy Dialogues with the help of the following suggestions. Those laity "signed up" should read Fenhagen's book, plus introduction to the Dialogue. Then read the Dialogue for each chapter prior to each meeting. Convenors should note the clergy experiences that will easily translate as is into lay experience. (For example, Chapter 1 will easily translate, Chapter 3 will not.) Then use this guide to make the translation from clergy to laity.

Chapter 1: Leadership in an Era of Turbulence
Under Focus #1 (Clergy Dialogue) do the first two exercises. You, from your lay perspective, "Think of an experience...of stability in a difficult situation and another experience that triggered a sense of discouragement in you, both in your congregation in the past year or so." Use wording in Dialogue. Share and discuss. Then choose another item from the Dialogue that especially involves you—the laity—and use the questions given. How do you feel it must be for clergy in the midst of so much change?

Chapter 2: A Profile of Episcopal Clergy
Do both Focus #1 and #2 from a lay perspective. The wellness checklist is based on clergy-family data, so skip over to the last discussion—what is needed in the church system to encourage thriving clergy, support those "at risk," and help clergy in trouble. How can you assist this to happen?

Chapter 3: Rethinking Our Theologies of Ordination
Using Focus #1, think of an experience of being at an ordination and what you saw and heard and felt the ritual was saying about the role of the ordained and its relationship with laity and congregations. (For those who have not been to an ordination, perhaps the installment of a new priest or ordained leader could be described and reflected on.)

Chapter 4: The Bishop and Diocese in a Time of Change.
Use Focus #1 if several of you did experience the bishop's (moderator's) visit. If not, explore some of the questions there—basically "who is the bishop for you and for your congregation?" What function or symbolic role does s/he have that you can see or appreciate? Can you imagine the bishop's chair becoming a symbol of presence rather than absence? How?

Chapter 5: The Case for Systemic Change
Do Focus #1 and #2, and under Focus #3 pick up on Fenhagen's description of why laity's ministry in the marketplace has never been fully embraced in the Episcopal Church and other denominations. Discuss his argument and conclusions.

Chapter 6: The Spiritual Roots of Christian Leadership
Focus #1. Perhaps entitlement and loneliness extend to the laity? Think of (and share) an experience when you felt an assumption or expectation of you by a clergyperson did not fit with your sense of who you are as a lay person and what you are called to be and do...You felt perhaps your vocation diminished, your role devalued?...Continue with the Dialogue questions—pick up on parts that are relevant as you have time. Then: How can laity and clergy clarify their assumptions and expectations of one another? Is it that we don't know how, or are afraid to offend? How you could open up your feelings about assumptions laid on you?

Candidate Screening Committees, Commissions on Ministry

30-minute reflections based on each of the six chapters.

Pre-work. All committee members read entire book, *Ministry for a New Time*. Then read the chapter "Dialogue" before the meeting at which it will be discussed. Try to appropriate the suggested "experiences for sharing" within the context of the commission on ministry.

Brief suggestions for the 30-minute exercises
Chapter 1: Given the "era of turbulence" do you seen signs of anxiety in the aspirants? What do you consider to be essential in the formation of

the aspirants? What do you consider to be essential in the formation of ordained people in a changing church? Chapter 2: How can we better recognize aspirants whose health and skills will give them the ability to "thrive" as ordained leaders? Chapter 3: Are we clear about our theology of ordination and how that "looks" in a well-functioning minister/priest? Chapter 4: How do you find aspirants responding to authority (bishop, screening committee, or procedures)? Chapter 5: What questions could you ask of the aspirants that get at their coping with, or initiating change? (They will have to do both as ordained ministers.) Chapter 6: "Entitlement" may start early. What questions could you ask about aspirants' sense of status, "different rule," that they may associate with the ordained role? For example, "How are other members of your congregation treating you now that you are seeking ordination? How do you feel about that?"

Church Boards, Vestries

The "annual retreat," be it a day or weekend, would be a good opportunity for selected Dialogues with Fenhagen's text. It will help build a team for the Vestry's task, especially if combined with goal setting and articulation of mutual expectations among members, clergy, and laity. Again all should read *Ministry for a New Time* and the Dialogues. Both clergy and laity can share some of the Dialogue experiences, relating them to their own leadership context. For example, in Chapter 1 Dialogue members of a vestry could share personal experiences of stability and discouragement in your work of congregational leadership...and ask themselves, "How is the congregation doing in these times of change? Are the challenges different for clergy, different for laity?" Some chapter Dialogues won't work as well, but can give ideas for translation needed for vestries and church boards. (Some of the laity interview also give ideas for bringing personal vocational experience to the text for the purpose of insight about ordained role, clergy-laity relationship, and the task of congregational leadership.)

The Alban Institute:
an invitation to membership

The Alban Institute, begun in 1974, believes that the congregation is essential to the task of equipping the people of God to minister in the church and the world. A multi-denominational membership organization, the Institute provides on-site training, educational programs, consulting, research, and publishing for hundreds of churches across the country.

The Alban Institute invites you to be a member of this partnership of laity, clergy, and executives—a partnership that brings together people who are raising important questions about congregational life and people who are trying new solutions, making new discoveries, finding a new way of getting clear about the task of ministry. The Institute exists to provide you with the kinds of information and resources you need to support your ministries.

Join us now and enjoy these benefits:

CONGREGATIONS: The Alban Journal, a highly respected journal published six times a year, to keep you up to date on current issues and trends.

Inside Information, Alban's quarterly newsletter, keeps you informed about research and other happenings around Alban. Available to members only.

Publications Discounts:

- ☐ 15% for Individual, Retired Clergy, and Seminarian Members
- ☐ 25% for Congregational Members
- ☐ 40% for Judicatory and Seminary Executive Members

Discounts on Training and Education Events

Write our Membership Department at the address below or call us at 1-800-486-1318 or 301-718-4407 for more information about how to join The Alban Institute's growing membership, particularly about Congregational Membership in which 12 designated persons receive all benefits of membership.

 The Alban Institute, Inc.
Suite 433 North
4550 Montgomery Avenue
Bethesda, MD 20814-3341